Advanced UX Writing

Best Practices for Engagement, Competition, and Conversion

Acknowledgment

I would like to begin by expressing my genuine appreciation to my significant other. Your guidance and feedback throughout the writing process were invaluable in shaping my ideas and refining my prose. Your keen eye for detail and deep understanding of UX writing has made this book much stronger and more impactful. I absolutely have to extend my heartfelt thanks to the talented team at Whook45. Your passion, expertise, and tireless efforts have been essential in bringing this book to life.

To my fellow UX writers and colleagues, I'm grateful for the many conversations and collaborations we've had over the years. Your insights and feedback have been instrumental in shaping my thinking and pushing me to be a better writer. Thank you for your support and camaraderie.

To my family and friends, I'm deeply appreciative of your unwavering support, encouragement, and love. You've been my rock throughout this journey, and I couldn't have done it without you.

Finally, to the readers of this book, thank you for your interest and support. I hope that this book will provide you with the tools, insights, and inspiration to help you become a better UX writer and practitioner. Your feedback and engagement are always welcome and appreciated.

Content

Chapter 1

Introduction

User experience (UX) writing is truly the bridge between users of modern technology designs and the product itself. As the digital world continues to evolve, the importance of UX writing has increased significantly. In essence, UX writing is the practice of creating written content that guides and assists users through an experience, making it more intuitive, seamless, and engaging. It is a crucial aspect of user-centered design, which places the user at the center of the design process, ensuring that their needs and goals are met.

The primary goal of UX writing is to make interactions with technology more human-like. While many people associate UX writing with digital products such as websites and apps, it extends beyond these platforms. UX writing can be found in a wide range of products and services, including smart home devices, digital assistants, chatbots, and even physical products that require user instructions.

To understand the importance of UX writing, it's important to first recognize the crucial role that language plays in communication. Language is the primary means by which we interact with the world around us, and it plays a critical role in shaping our perceptions and experiences. Effective language use can create an emotional connection with users, making them feel heard, understood, and valued. This emotional connection can lead to increased loyalty and brand affinity, and ultimately, drive business success.

UX writing can help bridge the gap between user expectations and technology capabilities. By using clear and concise language, UX writers can help users understand the features and functionality of a product, as well as how to use it effectively. Good UX writing can improve the user's overall experience, making it more intuitive, efficient, and enjoyable.

When it comes to accessibility, clear and concise language is essential for users with different abilities, particularly those with visual or cognitive impairments. Inclusivity and accessibility are critical components of user-centered design, and UX writing can play a significant role in ensuring that digital products and services are accessible to all users.

In recent years, the demand for UX writers has increased significantly. This growth can be attributed to the rise of digital products and services, as well as the recognition of the importance of user-centered design. According to a report by LinkedIn, UX writing was among the top 10 emerging jobs in 2020, with a 160% growth in job openings since 2015. Furthermore, the report states that

UX writers earn an average salary of $90,000 per year in the United States.

The potential of UX writing is vast, and its impact can be felt in many industries. From e-commerce to healthcare, financial services to education, UX writing can help organizations create better products and services that meet the needs and expectations of their users. Effective UX writing can help organizations improve their customer satisfaction, reduce support costs, and increase revenue.

One of the key characteristics of UX writing is its diversity. UX writers must have a deep understanding of their users' needs and goals, as well as the context in which they are using the product or service. This requires a diverse set of skills, including empathy, research, and collaboration.

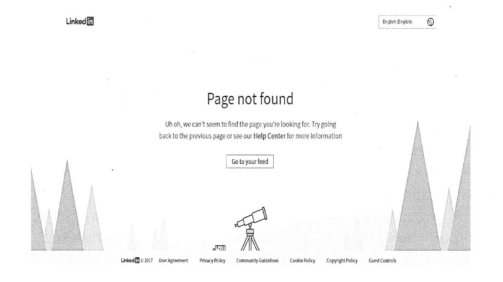

Linked[in]

English (English)

Page not found

Uh oh, we can't seem to find the page you're looking for. Try going back to the previous page or see our **Help Center** for more information

Go to your feed

Linked[in] © 2017   User Agreement   Privacy Policy   Community Guidelines   Cookie Policy   Copyright Policy   Guest Controls

Effective UX writing requires an understanding of the principles of user-centered design. This includes conducting user research to understand the user's goals and needs, creating personas to represent different user groups, and designing user flows and interactions that are intuitive and easy to use. UX writers must work closely with designers, developers, and product managers to ensure that the language used in the product is consistent, clear, and meets the needs of the user.

The role of UX writing is not limited to the creation of new products and services. It also plays a critical role in the ongoing maintenance and improvement of existing products. UX writers must constantly monitor user feedback and analytics to identify areas for improvement and make changes to the language used in the product accordingly.

As the field of UX writing continues to evolve, there have been various definitions coined by different groups. One of the most commonly cited definitions is by content strategist and UX writer, John Saito. He defines UX writing as "the act of crafting copy that guides users through an interface and helps them interact with it." This definition highlights the importance of language in guiding users through a digital experience, making it more intuitive and engaging.

Another definition comes from the Nielsen Norman Group, a leading research and consulting firm in the field of user experience. They define UX writing as "the practice of crafting the text that appears throughout a digital product to support its usability and define its personality." This definition emphasizes the importance of UX writing in shaping the user's perception of the product and creating an emotional connection with them.

Regardless of the specific definition, it's clear that UX writing plays a critical role in improving the user's experience with digital products and services. The language used in a product can have a significant impact on the user's emotions, perceptions, and behavior. Effective UX writing can create a sense of trust, clarity, and ease of use, while poor UX writing can lead to confusion, frustration, and ultimately, a negative user experience.

UX writing is used in various products and services. In each case, UX writing plays a critical role in creating a positive and engaging user experience, helping users achieve their goals, and ultimately driving business success. Here are some examples of how UX writing is applied in various products and services.

Airbnb

The UX writing on the Airbnb website and app plays a critical role in helping users navigate the platform, book accommodations, and manage their bookings. For example, when a user searches for a place to stay, the website or app provides clear, concise information about the property, including details about the amenities, location, and price.

Slack

UX writing in Slack helps users communicate with each other in a clear and effective way. The writing style is friendly, conversational, and often humorous, which creates a positive and engaging user experience. Slack also uses UX writing to provide users with clear instructions on how to use the platform, including how to set up channels, send messages, and share files.

Duolingo

UX writing plays a crucial role in helping users learn new languages through Duolingo's app. The writing is simple, direct, and easy to understand, which makes it easy for users to follow the lessons and exercises. Additionally, the app uses UX writing to provide users with feedback on their progress, encouraging them to continue learning and improving their language skills.

Spotify

UX writing in Spotify helps users discover new music, create playlists, and navigate the app's many features. For example, when a user searches for a specific song or artist, the app provides relevant recommendations based on their search history and listening habits. Additionally, the app uses UX writing to provide users with clear instructions on using features such as the "Discover Weekly" playlist or the "Daily Mix" feature.

Amazon

UX writing on Amazon helps users find and purchase products quickly and easily. The writing is clear, and concise, and provides users with all the information they need to make informed purchasing decisions. Additionally, the app uses UX writing to provide users with recommendations based on their search history and previous purchases, encouraging them to explore new products and categories.

Brand Tone and Voice

Voice and tone are essential components of UX writing that are often overlooked. These two elements are critical to creating a consistent and cohesive experience for users. Let's delve into the meanings of voice and tone and explore how they can be used to improve user experience. We will also look at how various brands have altered their voice and tone over the years to suit their customers' needs and how it has affected their business.

Voice and Tone Defined

Voice refers to the personality and values of a brand that shines through its content. It encompasses a brand's values, mission, and purpose, and is consistent across all its communication channels. A brand's voice can be described as its "personality" that differentiates it from its competitors. It's how a brand talks to its audience and how it makes them feel.

On the other hand, tone refers to the emotion and attitude of a brand's communication in a particular situation or context. It's how the brand conveys its voice and message to the user. Tone can be described as the "mood" of the content, and it can change depending on the context or user's state of mind. For example, a brand's tone may be friendly, informative, or formal, depending on the context.

Unique Characteristics of Voice and Tone

A brand's voice and tone should be unique and consistent across all communication channels. They should be recognizable and differentiate the brand from its competitors. A well-defined voice and tone can build trust and establish a connection between the brand and its users.

Voice and tone should also be tailored to the target audience. The language, style, and tone used to communicate with a young audience may differ from those used to communicate with an older audience. The tone used to communicate with a customer who has just had a positive experience with the brand may differ from the tone used to communicate with a customer who has had a negative experience.

Examples of Voice and Tone

Let's take a look at some examples of voice and tone in UX writing:

Mailchimp

Mailchimp, an email marketing company, is known for its fun and quirky voice that resonates with small business owners. The brand's tone is friendly, informal, and humorous, which is consistent across all its communication channels. For example, when a user forgets their password, Mailchimp's password reset email says, "Uh-oh.

We can't find your password. That's okay. We forget things, too. Let's get you a new one."

Apple

Apple is known for its sleek, minimalist design and straightforward, concise language. The brand's tone is confident, informative, and professional. Apple's website is an excellent example of the brand's voice and tone. The language used on the website is concise, and the messaging is clear. For example, when describing the iPhone's features, Apple states, "The world's most popular camera is even better." The statement is simple, yet it conveys confidence in the brand's product.

Slack

Slack, a communication platform for teams, has a straightforward and professional voice that resonates with its business audience. The brand's tone is informative, clear, and helpful. Slack's voice and tone are evident in its user onboarding process, where it provides clear instructions and explanations to help users get started. For example, when explaining how to use the platform, Slack states, "Start typing in the message field to begin a conversation. Your teammates will see your message in the channel and can respond in real-time."

Changing Voice and Tone to Suit Customer Needs

Brands often change their voice and tone to suit their customers' needs. For example, a brand may adopt a more casual tone when communicating with a younger audience or a more professional tone when communicating with a business audience.

One brand that has undergone a significant change in its voice and tone is Old Spice. Old Spice used to be known for its classic and straightforward marketing aimed at men. However, in 2010, Old Spice launched a new marketing campaign featuring a series of humorous ads aimed at a younger audience. The new ads featured a shirtless, muscular man delivering humorous one-liners about the product. The new campaign was a hit, and it generated a significant buzz on social media. The brand's new voice and tone resonated with a younger audience, and it helped to revitalize the brand.

Another example of a brand changing its voice and tone is Airbnb. When Airbnb first launched, the brand's voice and tone were focused on the platform's practical benefits, such as finding affordable accommodation while traveling. However, as the platform grew, Airbnb realized that its users were looking for more than just a place to stay. They were looking for unique experiences that would make their travels more memorable. To appeal to this audience, Airbnb changed its voice and tone to focus on the emotional benefits of using the platform. The brand's messaging now emphasizes the unique and personalized experiences that users can have while using Airbnb.

The Importance of Consistency

While changing voice and tone to suit customer needs can be beneficial, it's essential to maintain consistency across all communication channels. Inconsistencies in voice and tone can create confusion and erode trust between the brand and its users. A well-defined and consistent voice and tone can help to establish a strong brand identity and build trust with users.

"Changing voice and tone to suit customer needs can be beneficial, but it's important to maintain consistency across all communication channels. Inconsistencies in voice and tone can create confusion and erode trust between the brand and its users."

As a UX writer, it's important to remember that your writing has a significant impact on the user experience. A clear, concise, and consistent voice and tone can help users understand and navigate the product or service, while a confusing or inconsistent voice and tone can lead to frustration and distrust.

Here are some key takeaways for UX writers when it comes to voice and tone:

- **Define your brand's voice and tone:** Before you start writing, take the time to define your brand's voice and tone. Consider your target audience, your brand's values and personality, and your communication goals.

- **Tailor your voice and tone to your audience:** Your voice and tone should be tailored to your target audience. Use language, style, and tone that resonate with your audience and align with their needs and preferences.
- **Be consistent:** Consistency is key when it comes to voice and tone. Your voice and tone should be consistent across all communication channels, from your website to your social media accounts.
- **Be adaptable:** While consistency is important, it's also essential to be adaptable. As your brand evolves and your audience changes, you may need to adjust your voice and tone to stay relevant.
- **Test and iterate:** Finally, don't be afraid to test and iterate your voice and tone. Solicit feedback from users, track engagement metrics, and make adjustments as needed to ensure that your voice and tone are effective.

Defining your voice: Why is a Defined voice necessary?
A defined UX writing voice is important for several reasons:

Consistency in style

A consistent UX writing voice helps create a cohesive experience for users. When the same tone and style are used throughout a product, users can easily identify, trust, and understand the brand's values and message.

Clarity of information

A well-defined UX writing voice helps users understand the product and its features more easily. Clear and concise language makes it easier for users to complete tasks and achieve their goals.

Engages Target Audience

There is nothing as engaging as a voice that is suited to a specific demographic. Incorporating a voice that speaks for, inspires, motivates, informs, and entertains your target audience is one of the best strategies for client retention.

Eliminating competition

In the past, every product or service had a generic voice that was boring and cliché. Today, many brands seek to sound different, unique, and appealing enough to outwit the competition and take over the market.

Unique Personality

A UX writing voice can add personality to a product, making it more engaging and memorable. A unique and consistent voice can differentiate a brand from its competitors and help create a more emotional connection with users.

Branding

A defined UX writing voice is an essential part of branding. It helps to establish and reinforce a brand's values and personality, making it more recognizable and distinct in the market.

Steps to Defining your UX Writing Voice

Defining a UX writing voice is a critical step in establishing a brand identity and creating a consistent user experience. A UX writing voice is the personality, tone, and language used in a brand's digital content, such as product descriptions, microcopy, and user interface labels. It is important to define a consistent voice that resonates with the brand's target audience and reflects its values and mission. Here are the steps to defining your UX writing voice:

Establish brand identity and values

Before defining a writing voice, it is essential to understand the brand's identity and values. Conduct research and review the brand's mission statement, vision, and tone of voice guidelines. Identify the brand's key values and messaging, and ensure they align with the voice you intend to create. Skim through existing material that the brand currently has, discuss the target audience with the research team, and collect all relevant information. Try to be honest about your notes, do not exaggerate information, and do not be afraid to include the weaknesses of the product as this makes it human and relatable.

Don't just tell people that your products are great, be more detailed instead, tell them why your products are great and why they should be trusted. Invoke information when you speak, this appeal to the user and helps to build trust.

After gathering all the information you need, assess and eliminate the most irrelevant of all the information until you end up with the most essential values for your brand. Some of the following values can be used independently or as a combination of any number for a single product:

1. **Quality:** A brand that consistently delivers high-quality products or services can build a reputation for excellence and trustworthiness.
2. **Innovation:** Brands that push the boundaries of what's possible in their industry can create a sense of excitement and anticipation among their customers.
3. **Authenticity:** Brands that stay true to their core values and mission can create a strong emotional connection with their customers.

4. **Sustainability:** Brands that prioritize environmental and social responsibility can appeal to customers who value ethical and eco-friendly practices.
5. **Customer service**: Brands that prioritize customer satisfaction and go above and beyond to solve problems can earn a loyal following.
6. **Design:** Brands that invest in thoughtful, visually appealing design can stand out in crowded markets and create a strong brand identity.
7. **Affordability:** Brands that offer high-quality products or services at affordable prices can appeal to budget-conscious customers.
8. **Convenience:** Brands that make it easy for customers to find and purchase their products or services can build a reputation for reliability and accessibility.
9. **Community:** Brands that create a sense of belonging and foster connections among their customers can build a loyal following and drive word-of-mouth marketing.
10. **Reputation:** Brands that have a strong reputation for quality, trustworthiness, and reliability can enjoy sustained success over time.

Define the criteria for the writing voice

Once you have a clear understanding of the brand identity and values, it's time to establish the criteria for the writing voice. The criteria will serve as a guide to ensure the writing voice stays on-brand. Consider factors like the brand's personality, target audience, tone, and purpose.

You may start by drafting all the characteristics that are suited to your brand such as *Happy, positive, playful, caring, serious, attentive, smart, humble, curious, loyal, sarcastic, witty, humor,* and other interesting characteristics, and narrow down by picking 2 or 3 of the characters that closely defines your brand and would appeal best to its target audience.

For instance, let's combine "Witty", "Loyal", and "positive" in a 404 message for a website that sells shoes:

"Oops, it looks like you've stumbled upon a sole-searching conundrum! Our website is currently taking a breather, but fear not, we'll be back soon with a spring in our step. In the meantime, the link below and We'll see you on the other side of this error page with a fresh pair of kicks waiting for you!"

Now let's combine "curious," "playful", and "sarcasm" in a 404 message for a website that sells jewelry.

"Uh-oh! This page seems to be playing hide and seek. While we're on the hunt, why not check out our other dazzling gems? Who knows, you might find something even more captivating. Keep exploring and stay curious!"

Simple isn't it. As easy as it seems, there are rules to this. You obviously know that you cannot combine characteristics such as "Playful" "serious" and "sarcasm" as that would be a recipe for disaster. Users may misunderstand the message.

Here are a few rules to keep you on track:

Positive and Happy: your choice of words should be excited, never negative, highlight benefits, and use exclamations to celebrate successes.

Loyal and honest: Be sincere about the situation, and act in the interest of the user always.

Playful: Use jokes and funny references, be clear and easy to understand, and don't be formal or use negative emotions

Caring and attentive: Use short sentences to help those with short attention spans, use easy language, show respect, comfort the user by using phrases like "Don't worry", address users directly with personal pronouns.

Smart and curious: express genuine interest in the needs of the user, use short simple, and helpful information, and use intelligent questions to find out more information from users on how you can be of service.

Collect relevant information

Start by gathering information from various sources, including customer feedback, surveys, interviews, and analytics. Identify the language and phrases your customers use when describing your product or service, as this can influence your writing voice. Look for patterns and themes that reflect the brand's identity and values. This may seem a bit overwhelming all at once, but not to worry, we will touch on how to collect relevant information as we proceed.

Eliminate the irrelevant ones

Not all information collected will be relevant to the brand's writing voice. Review the data and eliminate any information that does not align with the brand's identity and values. Focus on the language and phrases that best reflect the brand's personality, tone, and purpose.

Isolate the information that makes up the brand's voice

Once you have collected and reviewed the data, isolate the information that makes up the brand's voice. This could include specific words, phrases, or sentence structures that align with the brand's identity and values. Establish a style guide that outlines the brand's writing voice criteria, including examples of language to use and avoid. We will take a look at how to create a style guide as we proceed.

Test and refine the writing voice

Test the writing voice in different contexts, such as social media, user interfaces, and marketing materials. Solicit feedback from stakeholders and customers and use analytics to measure its effectiveness. Refine the writing voice based on feedback and analytics, ensuring it continues to align with the brand's identity and values.

Chapter 2

What is a Style Guide and Why is it Necessary?

In the world of UX writing, a style guide is a crucial component of creating and maintaining a consistent and cohesive user experience. A style guide is a comprehensive set of guidelines and standards that dictate the tone, voice, and language used in all user-facing content. It is a reference document that provides a clear and consistent framework for writers, editors, and designers to follow, ensuring that all content produced is on-brand, user-friendly, and effective.

Many UX writing teams make the mistake of skipping the creation of a comprehensive style guide, because a style guide may be time-consuming and require quite a bit of brainstorming, however, style guides are probably the most important documents a design team can have. A style guide typically covers a wide range of topics, from grammar and punctuation to tone and style. It may include guidance on formattings, such as headings and subheadings, font sizes, and spacing. It may also include guidance on specific terms and phrases to be used (or avoided) in certain contexts, as well as guidance on tone and voice. The ultimate goal of a style guide is to create a clear and consistent user experience across all touchpoints, from websites and mobile apps to print materials and customer support interactions.

One of the key benefits of a style guide is that it helps to ensure consistency across a wide range of content types and platforms. For example, if a company produces content for a variety of different products, platforms, and audiences, a style guide can help to ensure that all content produced by the company is consistent and on-brand. This is particularly important for companies that have multiple writers and editors working on different projects, as it can be difficult to maintain a consistent voice and tone without clear guidelines.

In addition to promoting consistency, a style guide can also help to improve the overall quality of content. By providing clear guidance on grammar, punctuation, and style, a style guide can help to ensure that all content is written in a clear, concise, and user-friendly manner. This can help to improve user engagement and satisfaction, as users are more likely to engage with content that is easy to read and understand.

Another important benefit of a style guide is that it can help to reduce the amount of time and effort required to create new content. By providing a clear and comprehensive set of guidelines, a style guide can help to streamline the content creation process, making it faster and more efficient. This can be particularly important for companies that produce a large volume of content on a regular basis, as it can help to reduce the workload for writers and editors.

A style guide can also be a useful tool for onboarding new employees or contractors. By providing clear guidance on the company's voice, tone, and style, a style guide can help to ensure that new hires are able to quickly get up to speed and start producing high-quality content that is consistent with the company's brand and messaging.

A style guide can help to ensure that all content produced by a company is accessible and inclusive. By providing guidance on how to write content that is easy to read and understand, a style guide can help to ensure that all users, regardless of their level of literacy or cognitive ability, are able to engage with the content. This can help to promote a more inclusive and accessible user experience, which is increasingly important in today's digital landscape.

Welcome to the Mailchimp Content Style Guide

This style guide was created for Mailchimp employees, but we hope it's helpful for other content and communications teams too.

If you work at Mailchimp

This is our company style guide. It helps us write clear and consistent content across teams and channels. Please use it as a reference when you're writing for Mailchimp.

This guide goes beyond basic grammar and style points. It's not traditional in format or content. We break a number of grammar rules for clarity, practicality, or preference.

Here are a few companies that use content style guides:

1. Google
2. Microsoft
3. Dropbox
4. Airbnb
5. Shopify
6. IBM
7. Apple
8. Facebook
9. Amazon
10.   Uber
11.   Lyft
12.   PayPal
13.   LinkedIn

14.   Twitter
15.   Salesforce
16.   Slack
17.   HubSpot
18.   Atlassian
19.   Mailchimp
20.   Mozilla.

What makes up a good UX style guide?

A good UX writing style guide should establish clear guidelines for the language and tone used in user interfaces, ensuring a consistent and cohesive user experience. Here are some key elements that a UX writing style guide should include:

1. Tone and Voice: Define the tone and voice of your brand or product. This will help ensure consistency in the tone of your copy and create a consistent voice for your product.
2. Language: Establish guidelines for the language used in your product. This should include standards for spelling, grammar, and punctuation.
3. Writing Style: Define the writing style of your product. This includes guidelines for the use of active versus passive voice, the use of contractions, and the use of jargon or technical terms.

4. Content Structure: Establish guidelines for the structure of your content. This includes guidelines for headings, subheadings, and paragraphs.
5. Microcopy: Provide guidelines for writing microcopies, such as error messages, tooltips, and confirmation messages.
6. Accessibility: Ensure your language is inclusive and accessible to all users. This includes guidelines for avoiding ableist language and using plain language.
7. Brand Guidelines: Ensure your UX writing is consistent with your brand guidelines. This includes guidelines for logo usage, color schemes, and typography.
8. Tone in Context: Provide examples of how the tone should vary based on the context of the user interface. This includes guidelines for onboarding, error messages, and feedback prompts.

Remember, a good UX writing style guide is always evolving, so be sure to review and update it regularly to ensure that it remains relevant and effective.

Content of a style guide: Elements to Include in your Style Guide

Drafting a style guide for the first time can be a hassle if you are not completely sure of what should go in the pages and what should be left out. Here are the information specifics of a quality content style guide:

1. A style guide should include the basic UX writing criteria for quality

2. It should provide adequate information about inclusive and accessible UX writing

Universal design (noun)	**Accessibility** (adjective)	**Inclusive design** (verb)
A design that works for everyone in all scenarios and with every contingency	An attribute; a quality that makes an experience open to all	A human-centered design process that embraces diversity

3. It should contain specifics about the brand's voice and tone across various platforms

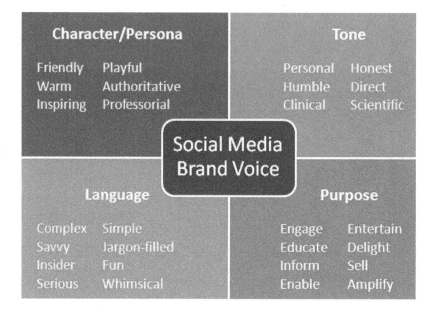

4. It should provide rules on how they should sound on various platforms, for instance, the difference between their social media writing style and their newsletter writing style.

Active voice

Use active voice. Avoid passive voice.

In active voice, the subject of the sentence does the action. In passive voice, the subject of the sentence has the action done to it.

- Yes: Marti logged into the account.
- No: The account was logged into by Marti.

Words like "was" and "by" may indicate that you're writing in passive voice. Scan for these words and rework sentences where they appear.

One exception is when you want to specifically emphasize the action over the subject. In some cases, this is fine.

- Your account was flagged by our abuse team.

5. It should also inform writers on how the brand prefers to spell certain words that are often written differently, such as e-book, E-book, and ebook.

You'll get on with all your co-workers and everyone at Mailchimp

We prefer the combined version of this word

⟶ coworkers

ⓧ Ignore

Creating your style guide step-by-step

Creating a UX writing style guide is an essential step in developing a consistent and effective user experience. It helps maintain consistency in language and tone throughout the product, ensuring that users receive clear and concise messaging. Here are the steps to creating your own UX writing style guide:

1. Identify your brand's voice and tone Your brand's voice and tone should be consistent with your company's personality and values. To determine your brand's voice and tone, you can ask yourself these questions:
- What is your brand's personality? Is it friendly, professional, humorous, or formal?
- What are your brand's core values? Is it innovation, honesty, or transparency?
- Who is your target audience? What are their demographics, interests, and pain points? Based on these answers, you can develop a clear and consistent voice and tone that resonates with your audience.

2. Define your writing style Once you have identified your brand's voice and tone, you need to define your writing style. Your writing style should be concise, clear, and easy to understand. Some factors to consider when defining your writing style include:
- Sentence length: Do you prefer long or short sentences?
- Jargon: Do you use industry-specific terms, or do you prefer to use plain language?
- Tone: Do you use contractions and colloquialisms, or do you prefer to use formal language?

- Capitalization: Do you capitalize product names, or do you prefer to use all lowercase? By defining your writing style, you ensure that all content is consistent and follows a specific set of guidelines.

3. Develop your content standards Content standards outline the specific rules and guidelines that writers must follow when creating content. These standards can include:
- Grammar and punctuation rules
- Formatting guidelines
- Tone and voice requirements
- Language and style preferences
- Brand-specific terminology By creating content standards, you ensure that all content follows a consistent style and tone, regardless of who is writing it.

4. Establish guidelines for accessibility and inclusivity Accessibility and inclusivity are essential components of UX writing. When creating your style guide, you should consider how to create content that is accessible to all users, regardless of their abilities. Some guidelines to consider include:
- Using clear and concise language
- Avoiding ambiguous phrasing
- Using descriptive link text
- Including alternative text for images
- Ensuring that color contrast meets accessibility standards By establishing guidelines for accessibility

and inclusivity, you create a better user experience for all users.

5. Provide examples and use cases Finally, to ensure that writers understand how to apply the style guide, you should provide examples and use cases. This can include:
- Examples of tone and voice
- Sample sentences that demonstrate the writing style
- Use cases for specific scenarios, such as error messages or calls to action By providing examples, you make it easier for writers to understand how to apply the guidelines and create content that is consistent with your brand's style and tone.

6. Review and refine your style guide After creating your style guide, it's important to review and refine it periodically. As your brand evolves, your writing style may need to evolve as well. Additionally, as you receive feedback from users and writers, you may identify areas where your style guide could be improved. Regularly reviewing and refining your style guide ensures that it remains relevant and effective.

7. Train your writers Once you have developed your style guide, you need to ensure that all writers and content creators understand and follow it. This can include:

- Conducting training sessions to introduce the style guide and its components
- Providing examples and use cases to demonstrate how to apply the guidelines
- Creating a reference guide or cheat sheet for quick access to the most important guidelines
- Encouraging feedback and questions to ensure that writers understand the guidelines and how to apply them

By training your writers, you ensure that all content is consistent with your brand's style and tone, regardless of who is creating it.

8. Implement and enforce your style guide Finally, it's important to implement and enforce your style guide. This can include:
- Conducting regular content audits to ensure that all content follows the guidelines
- Providing feedback to writers to ensure that they are following the guidelines
- Incorporating the style guide into your content creation process, such as through editorial reviews or peer editing
- Enforcing consequences for writers who consistently violate the guidelines

By implementing and enforcing your style guide, you ensure that all content is consistent with your brand's style and tone, and you create a better user experience for your users.

Style Guide Samples

Here are 2 samples of style guides for fictional companies called "Bronze Tech" and "Wear & Tear"

Bronze Tech Style Guide 2023

The Bronze Tech UX Writing Style Guide is a comprehensive document outlining the guidelines, rules, and specifications for all content creators to follow when creating content for our digital products. This guide will help ensure that all of our digital products have a consistent, engaging, and user-friendly user experience.

Tone and Voice

At Bronze Tech, we aim to create a tone and voice that is clear, concise, and professional yet engaging, friendly, and approachable. Our users should feel confident and comfortable using our digital products. Below are some key characteristics of our tone and voice:

- Clear and concise: Our users should be able to understand our content easily and quickly.

- Professional: We want to convey a sense of expertise and authority in our writing.
- Engaging and friendly: We want to build a connection with our users, making them feel comfortable using our products.

Examples:

- Clear and concise: Use bullet points to highlight key information.
- Professional: Use technical terms accurately and avoid using colloquial language.
- Engaging and friendly: Use humor and relatable language to connect with the user.

Content Guidelines

The following guidelines should be followed when creating content for our digital products:

1. Use active voice: Writing in active voice makes the content clearer, easier to read, and more engaging.

   Example: "Our app helps you manage your finances" instead of "Your finances can be managed by our app."

2. Keep sentences short: Shorter sentences are easier to read and understand.

   Example: "Our app tracks your expenses and income" instead of "Our app allows you to track your expenses and income."

3. Use simple language: Avoid using jargon or technical language that may not be familiar to our users.

   Example: "You can access your account by clicking the 'Login' button" instead of "You can authenticate your credentials by clicking the 'Login' button."

4. Use action-oriented language: Use language that prompts users to take action, creating a sense of urgency.

   Example: "Start saving now with our app" instead of "Our app can help you save money."

5. Be descriptive: Use descriptive language to help users understand the benefits of using our products.

   Example: "Our app provides you with detailed spending reports that help you identify areas, where you can save money" instead of "Our app, provides spending reports."

Punctuation and Formatting

1. Use proper punctuation: Use punctuation to convey meaning and clarity.

   Example: "Click on the 'Login' button, enter your username and password, and click 'Submit' to access your account."

2. Use headings and subheadings: Use headings and subheadings to break up content into smaller, easily digestible sections.

   Example: "Features" as a heading with "Expense Tracking" and "Budgeting" as subheadings.

3. Use bullet points: Use bullet points to highlight key information, making it easier to read and understand.

Example: "Key Features:

- Expense Tracking
- Budgeting
- Customizable Categories"

Conclusion

The Bronze Tech UX Writing Style Guide outlines the guidelines and specifications that should be followed when creating content for our digital products. Following these guidelines will ensure that our digital products have a consistent, user-friendly experience. Our tone and voice should be clear, concise, and professional yet engaging, friendly, and approachable. By following these guidelines, our content creators can help our users get the most out of our digital products.

Wear and Tear Style Guide 2023

The Wear and Tear UX writing style guide is designed to provide a consistent tone and voice to all content created for the company. This guide outlines the specific guidelines, rules, and best practices that writers should follow when creating content. By adhering to these guidelines, we can ensure that our customers have a seamless and enjoyable experience interacting with our brand.

Tone and Voice:

The tone and voice of Wear and Tear should be approachable, friendly, and casual. We want our customers to feel like they are talking to a friend when they interact with our brand. At the same time, we want to maintain a level of professionalism and expertise in the field of jeans.

Examples:

- **Approachable:** "Hey there! Looking for the perfect pair of jeans? We've got you covered!"
- **Friendly:** "We're so glad you're here! Let's find you the perfect fit."
- **Casual:** "No need to dress up, just throw on a pair of our jeans and you're good to go."

Guidelines:

- **Keep it concise:** Our customers are busy people. Keep the messaging clear and to the point.
- **Use active voice**: Active voice makes the content more engaging and easier to understand.
- **Write in the second person:** Address the customer directly using "you." This makes the content more personal and relatable.
- **Use descriptive language:** Describe the jeans in a way that paints a picture for the customer. Use sensory language to make the content more vivid and memorable.
- **Highlight the benefits:** Our customers want to know how our jeans will benefit them. Make sure to focus on the benefits and not just the features.
- **Use humor (sparingly):** A little humor can go a long way in making the content more memorable and engaging. However, be careful not to overdo it.

Punctuation and Writing Techniques:

- **Use contractions:** Contractions make the content more conversational and approachable.
- **Use bulleted lists:** Lists make the content easier to scan and digest.
- **Use the Oxford comma:** We use the Oxford comma to avoid any ambiguity in our messaging.
- **Use sentence case:** Capitalize the first letter of the first word in a sentence and proper nouns, but not every word in the sentence.

Example:

Looking for the perfect pair of jeans? You've come to the right place! Our jeans are designed to fit you like a glove, and they'll last you for years to come. Here are a few reasons why our jeans are the best:

- Made with high-quality denim that won't fade or wear out
- Designed with a flattering fit that hugs your curves in all the right places
- Available in a variety of colors and styles to match any outfit
- Affordable prices that won't break the bank

Conclusion:

The Wear and Tear UX writing style guide is designed to help writers create content that is approachable, friendly, and professional. By adhering to these guidelines, we can ensure that our customers have a seamless and enjoyable experience interacting with our brand. Remember to keep it concise, use an active voice, and highlight the benefits of our products.

Chapter 3

Collecting, Processing, and Documenting

The documentation phase of UX writing is often overlooked but remains one of the most important aspects in the creative process. As a writer or a designer, there is a need to document processes and keep track of changes made to designs as well as feedback from team members, clients, and stakeholders. There is often a lot of back and forth during the design phase where ideas are shared and edited. Teams brainstorm concepts and create drafts of their ideas and require an organized way to document them for present use or future reference. All of these contribute to the need for an effective information collection, and documentation process that not only allows proper storage of information but also allows team members such as developers, designers, and others to have access to the copies.

What is the importance of effective documentation in UX writing?

There are many reasons why writers need to ensure that their content is well documented. Here are some reasons to keep in mind.

1. Writers are able to keep a record of all text elements that have been used or are necessary for present and future use.
2. Documentation of text and content elements improves the consistency of voice and tone. It reminds the writer of previously used words, language, and terminologies used in the past. For instance, using the term "Sign up" becomes consistent and the writer does not mistakenly use "register" on any occasion.
3. It helps to organize the writer's work and make them organized for the designer or developer to use.
4. It makes translation seamless. In some cases the brand may decide to translate the content to a different language for inclusiveness, it becomes difficult to retain the exact language used previously if it wasn't documented. This inconvenience would mean that the developer has to start all over from scratch to rebuild the copy and design.

5. Documentation makes it easy to update existing copies. You would not have to go through extremely tedious processes to update the existing copies.
6. It provides a single database for your project and allows you to place all the texts, elements, and copies in one place rather than have them all scattered in various folders.

Requirement for Choosing a Documentation Method

Documentation is such a challenging but rewarding process. As useful as it is, many organizations generally do not bother with it because of its complexity. It is such uncharted territory that there is very little information on the internet about how to effectively document your copy let alone the right method for documentation. Let's take a look at the prerequisite for choosing the right method of documentation for your copy:

1. It should be time effective or else it would not be a smart method to use, especially when working with projects that are time bound.
2. It should be easily accessible to all parties involved and easy to share with team members.
3. It should have a restriction feature that allows you to create restrictions for different levels of access. For instance, the platform may give access to developers and restrict access to other non-tech team members.
4. It should be easy to include translated versions in case there is a need to add other languages
5. It should have adjustable features that align with the individual project needs

6. It should have accommodation for visual elements such as screenshots and not just text

Now we understand the criteria for choosing a documentation method, we still need to be clear on what to document. As a UX writer, there are typically two types of copy that require documentation, they are Alt texts and On-screen texts

What are Alt texts?

Alt text, short for "alternative text," is a description of an image in written form. In UX writing, alt text is used to ensure that images are accessible to people with visual impairments who may be using screen readers or other assistive technologies.

Here are some examples of alt text in UX writing:

1. Image of a dog playing in a park: "A brown and white dog playing fetch in a grassy park."
2. Image of a laptop with a blank screen: "A silver laptop with a blank screen and a keyboard."
3. Image of a person hiking in the mountains: "A person wearing a backpack and hiking boots standing on a rocky mountain trail with a view of the valley below."
4. Image of a cup of coffee on a table: "A white coffee mug with steam rising from it sitting on a wooden table."

5. Image of a bicycle leaning against a wall: "A red bicycle with a basket on the front leaning against a brick wall."

By providing descriptive alt text for images, UX writers can help ensure that all users have equal access to the content on a website or application.

What are On-screen text?

On-screen texts in UX writing refer to the words and phrases that appear on the interface of digital products such as websites, apps, or software. They are an essential part of the user experience as they guide the user and provide instructions, feedback, and information about the product.

Here are some examples of on-screen texts in UX writing:

1. Labels: Labels are the text that identifies the purpose or content of an element on the interface. For example, "Username," "Password," "Sign up," "Sign in," and "Search."
2. Headings and Subheadings: Headings and subheadings are used to organize content and make it easy to scan. For example, "Products," "Services," "About Us," and "Contact Us."
3. Error Messages: Error messages inform users when something has gone wrong, and provide information about how to fix the issue. For example, "Invalid email address," "Password must contain at least one

uppercase letter," and "Please fill in all required fields."

4. Buttons: Buttons are used to initiate actions or navigate to other parts of the interface. For example, "Submit," "Save," "Cancel," "Back," or "Next."

5. Tooltips: Tooltips provide additional information about an element or action when the user hovers over it. For example, "Click here to learn more," "Swipe left to delete."

6. Instructions: Instructions provide guidance on how to use a feature or complete a task. For example, "Drag and drop files here," "Select the date range for your report," and "Swipe right to accept."

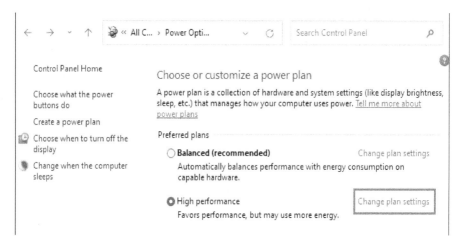

Criteria for Choosing Documentation Tool

Before choosing a tool for your documentation process, there are a few questions that must be answered and meetings that must be held with stakeholders to determine what their expectations are, the first set of questions are:

- What are the project requirements?

- Who and who would be working on the project, either individually or collaboratively?

- Who is allowed to give inputs during the project?

- Who are the stakeholders in the project?

Typically, the stakeholders are the designers, the product owners, the developers, the legal department, and the marketing department. Each of these stakeholders would contribute in different measures to the project and therefore should have access to the copy also in different measures. Whatever tool you decide to choose, it has to be one that can provide the stakeholders with visuals, sections to add comments, sections to make edits, and sections to approve or return for more editing.

It is usually advised to choose a tool that is trustworthy, easy to use, and inexpensive. You need to ensure that the tool allows access to as many people that need to use it as possible. Some tools have restrictions on the number of users, this of course would not be the best. The tool has to be open for as many accounts as possible and should be able to sync with various design tools.

The next step is to set up your tool and adjust its features to match the workflow and products. After that, test your tool to be sure of its efficiency and to see how it meets the overall requirements of project collaboration.

Documentation tools and uses

There are three main documentation methods used in UX writing, they are: in-Design, Customized, and Tool-based methods

In-Design

InDesign is a powerful desktop publishing software developed by Adobe that is commonly used for designing layouts for print and digital media. While it is not typically considered a tool for UX writing, it can be a useful tool for creating and organizing documentation for user experience design.

Here are some potential uses, pros, and cons of using InDesign for UX writing documentation:

Uses:

- Creating and formatting style guides: InDesign's layout tools can be helpful for creating and organizing style guides that outline the tone, voice, and style of a brand or product. It can also be used to document guidelines for visual elements like typography, color, and iconography.

- Designing user manuals and instructions: InDesign can be used to create detailed user manuals or instructional materials, complete with illustrations, diagrams, and other visual aids. These materials can be printed or distributed digitally.
- Compiling reports and presentations: InDesign can be used to compile research findings, user testing results, or other data into reports or presentations that can be easily shared with stakeholders.

Pros:

- Layout tools: InDesign's layout tools can help create polished and visually appealing documents that are easy to navigate and read.
- Integration with other Adobe tools: If your team already uses other Adobe tools like Photoshop or Illustrator, using InDesign can streamline your workflow and make it easier to integrate visuals into your documentation.
- Flexibility: InDesign can handle a wide variety of document types, from simple one-page guides to more complex manuals or presentations.

Cons:

- Learning curve: InDesign can be complex and may require some training to use effectively.

- Cost: InDesign is a paid tool, so it may not be accessible to teams with limited budgets.
- Limited collaboration tools: While InDesign has some collaboration features, they may not be as robust as other tools designed specifically for collaboration, like Google Docs or Confluence.

Overall, InDesign can be a useful tool for creating and organizing UX writing documentation, particularly for teams that already use Adobe tools and are comfortable with their workflow. However, it may not be the best option for teams on a tight budget or those who require robust collaboration features.

Another tool option that is widely used by UX writers is Figma.

Figma for Documentation

Figma is a popular design tool used for creating user interfaces, digital products, and other visual design projects. Figma has gained popularity in recent years due to its collaborative features, including real-time editing and commenting, as well as its ability to create and share design systems.

While Figma is primarily a visual design tool, it also has features that can be useful for UX writing. UX writing is the practice of creating clear and concise text that helps users interact with a product or service.

Here are some ways that Figma can be used for UX writing:

1. Designing and Prototyping User Flows: Figma can be used to create wireframes and prototypes of user flows, which can include UX writing such as labels, headings, and instructions. By creating a prototype, UX writers can test the clarity and effectiveness of their writing in context.

2. Collaborating with Designers: Figma's collaborative features make it easy for UX writers to work with

designers and other team members. They can share their work, make comments and revisions, and get feedback in real time.

3. Creating and Sharing Design Systems: Figma's design systems feature allows teams to create a library of design elements and components that can be reused across projects. This can include pre-written UX copy that can be easily implemented into new designs.

4. Integrations with Other Tools: Figma integrates with a variety of other tools, such as Jira and Slack, making it easy to track tasks and communicate with team members.

Pros:

- Collaborative features make it easy to work with designers and other team members
- Design systems can help ensure consistency across projects and improve efficiency
- Real-time editing and commenting make it easy to get feedback and make revisions quickly

Cons:

- While Figma can be used for UX writing, it is primarily a visual design tool, so it may not have all the features that UX writers need.
- Figma is a cloud-based tool, which may not be ideal for organizations with strict data security requirements.

Figma is a powerful design tool that can be used for UX writing. Its collaborative features, design systems, and integrations make it a great choice for teams that want to work together efficiently and effectively. However, it may not be the best tool for organizations with specific UX writing needs or those with strict data security requirements.

Now let's compare In-design to Figma and see what advantages they may have over one another.

Comparison	Figma	InDesign
Primary Use	User Interface (UI) and User Experience (UX) Design	Print and Digital Layout Design
Collaboration	Collaborative design tool that allows for real-time collaboration and commenting	Collaboration features are limited
Platform	Web-based	Desktop-based
File Formats	Figma files (.fig)	Adobe InDesign files (.indd)
Export Formats	SVG, PNG, JPG, PDF	PDF, EPS, SWF, HTML, XML
Learning Curve	Easy to learn and use	Requires some time to learn and use effectively
Cost	Free plan available, paid	Requires Adobe Creative

Comparison	Figma	InDesign
	plans start at $12 per editor per month	Cloud subscription, plans start at $20.99 per month

In summary, Figma is a web-based collaborative design tool primarily used for UI/UX design, while InDesign is a desktop-based layout design software used for print and digital design. Figma has an easier learning curve and offers more export formats, while InDesign offers more file formats and is more expensive, requiring a Creative Cloud subscription.

Tool-based Documentation

Tool-based documentation refers to the use of software tools to create and manage documentation. These tools can help UX writers to create, organize, and maintain documentation for various design projects. Here are some of the tools available for documentation in UX writing:

1. **Google Docs:** Google Docs is a popular tool for collaborative writing and documentation. It allows UX writers to work on the same document simultaneously and enables easy sharing and commenting on the content.

2. **Microsoft Word:** Microsoft Word is another widely used tool for documentation. It offers a range of formatting options, and its track changes feature enables easy review and editing of the content.

3. **Confluence:** Confluence is a powerful tool for documentation, especially for teams working on large projects. It offers features such as real-time collaboration, version control, and task management.

4. **Trello:** Trello is a visual project management tool that can be used for documentation. UX writers can create boards and cards to organize their content and collaborate with their team members.

5. **Notion:** Notion is a versatile tool that can be used for documentation, project management, and collaboration. It offers a range of templates, including ones specifically for UX writing.

6. **GitHub:** GitHub is a code hosting platform that can be used for documentation. UX writers can use it to create and manage documentation for design projects, collaborate with developers, and track changes to the content.

7. **Adobe XD:** Adobe XD is a design tool that can be used for creating wireframes, prototypes, and documentation. It offers features such as artboards, layers, and symbols to help UX writers organize their content.

8. **Sketch:** Sketch is another design tool that can be used for creating wireframes, prototypes, and documentation. It offers a range of plugins and templates to help UX writers streamline their workflow.

9. **Miro:** Miro is a collaborative online whiteboard that can be used for documentation. UX writers can use it to create diagrams, flowcharts, and other visual aids to support their content.

10. **Lucidchart**: Lucidchart is a diagramming tool that can be used for creating flowcharts, wireframes, and other visual aids for documentation. It offers a range of templates and shapes to help UX writers create professional-looking diagrams.

There are many tools available for documentation in UX writing, each with its own set of features and benefits. UX writers can choose the tool that best suits their needs and preferences to create high-quality documentation for their design projects.

Custom-made Documentation

Custom-made documentation in UX writing refers to creating a system for documenting and tracking copywriting in a consistent and organized way. One common method for doing this is by using a spreadsheet to document copies. Here are some pros and cons to consider when using this approach:

Pros:

1. Easy organization: Using a spreadsheet to document copies can be a convenient way to keep track of all the different copies you are working on in one place. It's easy to add new copies, make updates, and keep everything organized in a consistent format.
2. Clear communication: When you use a spreadsheet to document copies, it makes it easier to communicate with others involved in the project. Everyone can see what copy is being used, what changes have been made, and what still needs to be done.
3. Standardization: Using a spreadsheet to document copies helps to ensure that all copies are written in a consistent tone, voice, and style. This can help to maintain brand consistency and improve the overall user experience.
4. Easy to use: Writers who are non-tech staff can easily start using spreadsheets immediately without

the delays of spending time learning new apps and mastering collaborations on every new innovative app that is introduced.

5. They are budget-friendly: Spreadsheets are great for companies with very low operation budget. The software is free and does not require subscriptions

Cons:

1. It doesn't easily integrate with other design tools
2. It requires more effort to share copies compared to other modern tools
3. It has little to no aesthetics
4. It often gets crowded

Let's look at a few examples for custom-made documentation:

Screen/Feature	Copy	Notes/Context	Writer	Reviewer	Approval Status
Login Screen	"Welcome back! Please enter your email and password to continue."	User sees this screen after tapping "Login" button.	Jane	Bob	Approved
Error Message	"Invalid email or password. Please try	User sees this message when they input	Tom	Sarah	Needs revision

Screen/Feature	Copy	Notes/Context	Writer	Reviewer	Approval Status
	again."	incorrect login information.			
Checkout	"Review your order and confirm payment information."	User sees this screen after adding items to their cart.	Jane	Bob	Approved
Confirmation	"Your order has been confirmed. Thank you for your purchase!"	User sees this message after completing checkout.	Tom	Sarah	Pending approval

In this example, we have a table with several columns: Screen/Feature, Copy, Notes/Context, Writer, Reviewer, and Approval Status. Each row represents a specific piece of UX writing, such as copy for a login screen or an error message.

The "Screen/Feature" column specifies the screen or feature that the copy is associated with. The "Copy" column contains the actual text that the UX writer has written. The "Notes/Context" column provides additional context or instructions for the writer or reviewer. The "Writer" column shows the person who wrote the copy, while the "Reviewer" column shows the person responsible for reviewing the copy.

The "Approval Status" column indicates the status of the copy. In this example, we have three possible statuses: "Approved," "Needs revision," and "Pending approval." This column can be used to track the progress of the UX writing and ensure that it has been properly reviewed and approved before being implemented in the product.

By using a spreadsheet like this, teams can collaborate on UX writing and keep track of the status of each piece of copy, making it easier to ensure that the product's messaging is consistent and effective.

Lets look at something a bit more complex:

Screen/ Feature	Copy	Notes/ Context	Writer	Reviewer	Approval Status	Localization Status	Date Created	Date Updated
Login Screen	"Welcome back! Please enter your email and password to	User sees this screen after tapping "Login"	Jane	Bob	Approved	Not localized	2022-01-15	2022-01-15

Screen/ Feature	Copy	Notes/ Context	Writer	Reviewer	Approval Status	Localization Status	Date Created	Date Updated
	continue."	button.						
Error Message	"Invalid email or password. Please try again."	User sees this message when they input incorrect login information.	Tom	Sarah	Needs revision	Not localized	2022-01-15	2022-01-16
Checkout	"Review your order and confirm payment information."	User sees this screen after adding items to their cart.	Jane	Bob	Approved	Not localized	2022-01-16	2022-01-16
Confirmation	"Your order has been confirmed. Thank you for your purchase!"	User sees this message after completing checkout.	Tom	Sarah	Approved	Not localized	2022-01-16	2022-01-16
Signup Screen	"Create an account to get started."	User sees this screen after tapping "Signup" button.	Jane	Bob	Approved	Not localized	2022-01-17	2022-01-17

Screen/ Feature	Notes/ Copy	Context	Writer	Reviewer	Approval Status	Localization Status	Date Created	Date Updated
Success Message	"Your account has been created. Please check your email for verification instructions."	User sees this message after successfully creating an account.	Tom	Sarah	Approved	Not localized	2022-01-17	2022-01-18
Billing Info	"Enter your billing information below."	User sees this screen after selecting "Billing" from the menu.	Jane	Bob	Approved	Not localized	2022-01-18	2022-01-18
Contact Us	"Please fill out the form below to contact us."	User sees this screen after selecting "Contact Us" from the menu.	Tom	Sarah	Approved	Not localized	2022-01-19	2022-01-19

This table includes additional columns to track the localization and versioning of the UX writing.

The "Localization Status" column indicates whether the copy has been translated into other languages and, if so, the status of those translations. This information can be useful for teams working on multi-language products or those looking to expand their product into new markets.

The "Date Created" and "Date Updated" columns provide information on when each piece of UX writing was initially created and when it was last updated. This information can be useful for tracking the history of the copy and identifying any potential issues or inconsistencies.

Overall, this more complex spreadsheet can help teams to better manage their UX writing by tracking its status, localization, and versioning, while also providing important historical context.

Chapter 4

Integrating UX Writing into AGILE Processes

In today's fast-paced world, Agile methodologies have become increasingly popular. Agile is an iterative approach to software development, emphasizing flexibility, adaptability, and customer involvement. It's designed to help teams deliver software faster, with greater quality and efficiency. UX writing is an integral part of the Agile development process, and in this chapter, we'll explore how it works.

What is Agile?

Agile is an iterative and incremental approach to software development. It involves breaking down a project into small, manageable pieces called user stories, which are then completed in short iterations, usually lasting two to four weeks. At the end of each iteration, the team delivers a working product that can be tested and reviewed by stakeholders, including the end-users. The team then uses the feedback to improve the product and prioritize new features for the next iteration.

The Agile approach values working software over comprehensive documentation, customer collaboration over contract negotiation, and responding to change over following a plan. It's a flexible approach that allows teams to adapt to changing requirements, scope, and priorities.

Agile design process phases

The Agile development process involves four main phases: planning, execution, review, and retrospective. Here's an overview of each phase:

Planning

In the planning phase, the team identifies the product's goals, features, and user stories. The team creates a product backlog, a prioritized list of features, and user stories that need to be completed.

Execution

In the execution phase, the team works on the user stories identified in the product backlog. The team breaks down the user stories into smaller tasks and estimates how long each task will take to complete. The team then works on the tasks, using Agile methodologies such as Scrum or Kanban to manage the work.

Review

In the review phase, the team demonstrates the working product to stakeholders, including the end-users. Stakeholders provide feedback on the product, which the team uses to improve the product in the next iteration.

Retrospective

In the retrospective phase, the team reflects on the iteration and identifies what went well and what could be improved. The team uses this information to improve the process for the next iteration.

How is UX writing integrated into the Agile process?

UX writing is an essential part of the Agile process. It involves creating the content that appears in the user interface, such as button labels, error messages, and onboarding screens. UX writing is critical because it helps users understand how to use the product and what to expect from it.

UX writers are integrated into the Agile process in several ways. First, they collaborate with designers and developers to create user stories. UX writers provide input on the language and tone that should be used in the user interface, and they help ensure that the user stories are written in a way that is clear and understandable to the end users.

During the execution phase, UX writers work closely with designers and developers to ensure that the user interface content is integrated seamlessly into the product. UX writers provide the copy for buttons, forms, and other interface elements, and they work with the design team to ensure that the content is presented in a way that is visually appealing and easy to understand.

In the review phase, UX writers participate in user testing and feedback sessions. They use the feedback from the end-users to refine the product's language and ensure that it meets the user's needs.

In the retrospective phase, UX writers reflect on the iteration and identify areas where the language could be improved. They work with the team to develop best practices for writing content that is clear, concise, and user-friendly.

Collaborations between UX writers, designers, and developers

Effective collaboration between UX writers, designers, and developers is critical to the success of an Agile project. Collaboration starts with creating user stories that are clear and concise, so that everyone on the team understands what is being built and why. UX writers, designers, and developers should work together to create user stories that are focused on the user's needs and goals.

During the execution phase, UX writers collaborate with designers and developers to ensure that the content is integrated seamlessly into the product. Designers may provide wireframes or prototypes that the UX writer can use as a guide when creating the copy. Developers may provide feedback on how the content will be implemented, which can help the UX writer ensure that the content is technically feasible.

Throughout the process, UX writers, designers, and developers should communicate regularly to ensure that the content is meeting the user's needs and goals. If changes are needed, the team should collaborate to make those changes quickly and efficiently.

Best practices for UX writing in Agile projects

To ensure that UX writing is integrated effectively into the Agile process, there are several best practices that UX writers should follow. Here are some of the most important ones:

1. Collaborate early and often: UX writers should be involved in the project from the beginning, collaborating with designers and developers to create clear and concise user stories. They should also be involved in the review and retrospective phases, working with the team to refine the language and ensure that it meets the user's needs.

2. Keep it simple: In Agile projects, there is no room for overly complicated language or messaging. UX writers should strive to keep the language simple and easy to understand, using plain language whenever possible.

3. Be consistent: Consistency is key in UX writing. UX writers should establish style guidelines for the project and ensure that all content is written in a consistent style and tone.

4. Test and iterate: UX writers should be involved in user testing and feedback sessions, using the feedback to refine the language and ensure that it meets the user's needs. They should also be willing to iterate on the content as needed, making changes quickly and efficiently.

5. Emphasize user needs: The focus of UX writing in Agile projects should always be on the user's needs and goals. UX writers should strive to create content that is user-focused, using language that is clear and understandable to the end-users.

Role of UX Writer in AGILE Projects

As a UX writer, it's important to understand how to manage UX writing in agile projects, where development and design teams work together in sprints to deliver incremental product improvements. Let's look at the management and collaboration process with teams using illustrations and best practices, as well as the collaborative techniques used to include the UX writer in agile projects.

Agile development involves the constant iteration and improvement of products. Teams work in short sprints, typically 1-4 weeks long, to deliver incremental improvements to the product. During each sprint, the team collaborates to define and prioritize the features that will be delivered, and then work together to design, develop, test, and release those features.

The role of the UX writer in an agile project is to ensure that the content and language used in the product are clear, concise, and consistent, and that they support the overall user experience. The UX writer works closely with the design and development teams to ensure that the content is integrated into the design and functionality of the product.

Managing UX Writing in Agile Projects

To manage UX writing in agile projects, it's important to establish a clear process for collaboration and communication. Here are some best practices to consider:

1. Start with a content strategy:

Before the project begins, work with the team to establish a content strategy that aligns with the product goals and user needs. This will help ensure that the content is consistent and effective across the product.

2. Attend sprint planning and stand-up meetings:

Attend sprint planning meetings to help define the goals and priorities for each sprint, and stand-up meetings to stay informed about the team's progress and to identify any issues that need to be addressed.

3. Work in sprints:

Like the rest of the team, work in sprints to deliver incremental improvements to the product. Identify the content that needs to be delivered in each sprint and collaborate with the team to ensure that it's integrated into the design and functionality of the product.

4. Use collaboration tools:

Use collaboration tools like JIRA or Trello to stay organized and to communicate with the team. These tools can help you track progress, assign tasks, and communicate with the team in real-time.

5. Conduct regular content reviews:

Conduct regular content reviews to ensure that the content is clear, concise, and effective. Use metrics like user engagement, feedback, and analytics to inform your decisions.

Collaborating with Teams in Agile Projects

Collaboration is key to success in agile projects. Here are some collaborative techniques to include the UX writer in agile projects:

1. Attend design and development meetings:

Attend design and development meetings to stay informed about the product and to provide input on the content. This will help ensure that the content is integrated into the design and functionality of the product.

2. Work with the design team:

Work with the design team to ensure that the content is visually integrated into the design. Collaborate with the team to establish a style guide that outlines the tone, voice, and style of the content.

3. Work with the development team:

Work with the development team to ensure that the content is integrated into the functionality of the product. Collaborate with the team to establish content standards for the product, such as character counts, formatting rules, and error messages.

4. Use user stories:

Use user stories to identify the user needs that the content needs to support. This will help ensure that the content is aligned with the user's needs and goals.

5. Conduct usability testing:

Conduct usability testing to gather feedback on the content and identify areas for improvement. Use this feedback to inform your decisions and to make adjustments to the content as needed.

There are many ways to effectively manage the collaboration process with the development team to ensure that the UX writer is always up-to-date on the progress of the project and can easily synchronize their work with the design team, and that is with the use of the KANBAN BOARD.

As a UX writer, it's important to have a clear understanding of the project's progress and what needs to be done in order to meet the deadline. One way to achieve this is by using a Kanban board. Kanban is a project management methodology that emphasizes visualizing work, limiting work in progress, and improving workflow. A Kanban board is a physical or digital board that displays the progress of work items across different stages of the workflow. Let's explore how the Kanban board is used by the UX writer and other members of the team in Agile projects for collaboration.

How the Kanban Board Works

A Kanban board consists of a series of columns that represent the different stages of the workflow, such as To-Do, In Progress, and Done. Work items are represented by cards that are moved from one column to the next as they progress through the workflow. The board serves as a visual representation of the progress of the project and allows team members to easily see what needs to be done, what is currently being worked on, and what has been completed.

The Benefits of Using a Kanban Board

The use of a Kanban board has several benefits for Agile teams. Here are some of the key benefits:

1. Visualizing work - The Kanban board provides a visual representation of the progress of the project, which makes it easier for team members to understand what needs to be done and what has already been accomplished.
2. Limiting work in progress - The Kanban board encourages teams to limit the number of work items in progress at any given time, which helps to prevent bottlenecks and ensures that work is completed in a timely manner.
3. Improving workflow - By visualizing the workflow, teams can identify inefficiencies and make improvements to the process.
4. Enhancing collaboration - The Kanban board provides a shared visual space where team members can collaborate and communicate about the project's progress.

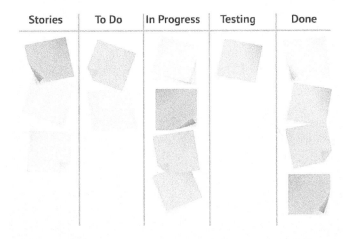

KANBAN BOARD

Stories	To Do	In Progress	Testing	Done

How the UX Writer Uses the Kanban Board

As a UX writer, the Kanban board can be a valuable tool for managing the content creation process. Here are some ways that the UX writer can use the Kanban board:

Creating content cards

The UX writer can create content cards for each piece of content that needs to be created. These cards can include information such as the content type, audience, and key messaging.

Moving cards through the workflow

The UX writer can move content cards through the different stages of the workflow, such as writing, editing, and approval. This allows the writer to easily track the progress of each piece of content.

Collaborating with other team members

The Kanban board provides a shared visual space where the UX writer can collaborate with other team members, such as designers and developers. For example, the writer can use the board to request images or other assets needed for the content.

Here are some examples of how the Kanban board is used by Agile teams:

1. **Content Creation** - A team of UX writers, designers, and developers are working on a website redesign project. The UX writers use the Kanban board to manage the content creation process. They create content cards for each page of the website and move the cards through the different stages of the workflow. The designers and developers can see the progress of the content creation and provide feedback as needed.

2. **Sprint Planning** - A team is planning for their upcoming sprint. They use the Kanban board to identify the user stories that will be included in the sprint and to assign tasks to team members. The board allows the team to see what needs to be done and who is responsible for each task.

3. **Bug Tracking** - A development team is working on a software product. They use the Kanban board to

track bugs and issues that have been reported by users. The board allows the team to see which issues are a priority and to track the progress of each issue as it moves through the workflow.

4. **Product Roadmap** - A product team is using the Kanban board to manage their product roadmap. The board includes cards for each feature or enhancement that is planned for the product, along with information about the priority, estimated effort, and expected delivery date. The board allows the team to see the big picture of the product roadmap and to track progress towards their goals.

5. **Marketing Campaigns** - A marketing team is using the Kanban board to manage their campaigns. The board includes cards for each campaign, along with information about the target audience, messaging, and marketing channels. The board allows the team to see which campaigns are currently in progress, which are planned for the future, and which have been completed.

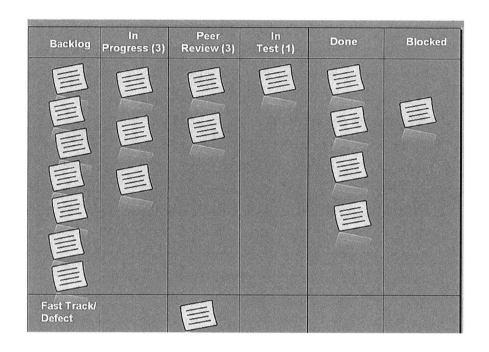

Here are a few examples of how to name your rows on a Kanban board

Row Name	Description
Backlog	This row contains all the tasks that are yet to be prioritized for implementation.
Ready for Dev	This row contains tasks that have been prioritized and are ready for development.
In	This row contains tasks that are currently being

Row Name	Description
Progress	worked on by the development team.
Testing	This row contains tasks that have been completed by the development team and are being tested for quality assurance purposes.
Review	This row contains tasks that have been tested and are awaiting review and approval from stakeholders.
Done	This row contains tasks that have been reviewed and approved by stakeholders and are considered complete.

Another Example:

Row Name	Description
Backlog	This row contains all the new ideas, feature requests, and user stories that are yet to be prioritized for implementation.
Ready for Design	This row contains tasks that have been prioritized and are ready to be designed.

Row Name	Description
Design In Progress	This row contains tasks that are currently being designed by the design team.
Ready for Dev	This row contains tasks that have been designed and are ready for development.
Development	This row contains tasks that are being developed by the development team.
Ready for Testing	This row contains tasks that have been completed by the development team and are ready for testing.
Testing	This row contains tasks that are being tested by the quality assurance team.
Ready for Review	This row contains tasks that have passed testing and are ready for review by stakeholders.
Review In Progress	This row contains tasks that are currently being reviewed by stakeholders.
Done	This row contains tasks that have been reviewed and approved by stakeholders and are considered complete.

The Kanban board is a valuable tool for Agile teams, including UX writers, to manage their workflow and collaborate effectively. By visualizing work, limiting work in progress, and improving workflow, the Kanban board can help teams to work more efficiently and effectively. As a UX writer, using a Kanban board can help you to track the progress of your content creation process, collaborate with other team members, and ensure that you meet your project deadlines.

Chapter5

Exploratory User Research and Testing for UX Writing

Exploratory user research and testing play an essential role in UX writing, it involves gathering data and insights from users to understand their needs, preferences, and behaviors, which can then be used to develop effective user-centric content. The process of exploratory user research and testing can involve various methods, such as surveys, user interviews, usability testing, and analytics data analysis. We will discuss the importance of exploratory user research and testing in UX writing and how it works.

Importance of Exploratory User Research and Testing in UX Writing:

1. **Understand User Needs:** Exploratory user research and testing allow UX writers to gather information about user needs and preferences. This information is critical to creating content that is relevant and useful to the target audience. Understanding user

needs also helps UX writers to develop content that is easy to read, understand, and navigate.

2. **Improve User Experience**: Exploratory user research and testing provide UX writers with insights into user behaviors and interactions with a product or service. By understanding how users interact with content, UX writers can develop content that enhances the user experience and meets their needs.

3. **Increase Engagement:** Well-crafted content can increase user engagement and retention. Exploratory user research and testing can help UX writers understand what type of content is most engaging to users, and how to present that content in a way that encourages users to interact with it.

4. **Ensure Accessibility:** Exploratory user research and testing can help UX writers ensure that their content is accessible to all users, regardless of their abilities. By understanding how users with different abilities interact with content, UX writers can develop content that is easy to understand and navigate for all users.

How Exploratory User Research and Testing Works in UX Writing:

1. **Surveys:** Surveys are an effective way to gather data on user preferences, needs, and behaviors. UX writers can use surveys to ask users about their content preferences, what types of information they

find most useful, and how they prefer to interact with content.

2. **User Interviews:** User interviews provide an opportunity for UX writers to gather more detailed information about user needs, preferences, and behaviors. During user interviews, UX writers can ask open-ended questions to understand user perspectives on specific topics or products.

3. **Usability Testing:** Usability testing involves observing users as they interact with a product or service. UX writers can use usability testing to observe how users interact with content, what problems they encounter, and how they navigate the content.

4. **Analytics Data Analysis:** Analytics data analysis involves analyzing data from user interactions with a product or service. UX writers can use analytics data to understand user behaviors, such as which pages are most frequently visited, how long users spend on each page, and what actions they take on each page.

The information acquired from these methods helps to develop information architecture of the product, this allows the UX writer to define the voice and tone as well as other needs. Let's start by taking a closer look at user research and some very critical user research methods for UX writing

User research refers to the process of gathering information and feedback from users to inform the creation of effective and user-friendly content. This research is conducted to better understand the needs, behaviors, and preferences of users and to identify areas where content can be improved.

The goal of user research in UX writing is to ensure that the content is easy to read, understand, and use for the target audience. This can involve conducting surveys, interviews, usability testing, and other methods to gather feedback from users.

User research helps UX writers to create content that is more user-centered, which can ultimately lead to higher engagement, better user experiences, and increased user satisfaction. By using user research, UX writers can create content that is tailored to the specific needs of their target audience and can ensure that the content is effective in meeting the user's goals.

Qualitative and Quantitative Research

Qualitative and quantitative researches are both important methods used in UX writing to understand user needs and behavior. Here's a breakdown of both:

Qualitative research involves gathering insights and feedback from a small group of users through methods like interviews, surveys, and usability testing. This type of research focuses on exploring and understanding the user's experience and can help UX writers identify pain points and areas where users may struggle with language or messaging.

Quantitative research, on the other hand, involves collecting numerical data from a large sample size. This type of research is useful for gathering statistics on user behavior, such as how often users click on a particular button or how many users complete a specific task. Quantitative research is often conducted through analytics tools or A/B testing.

Both qualitative and quantitative research can be used in UX writing to inform decisions about the language, tone, and messaging used in a product or service. For example, qualitative research may reveal that users struggle to understand a certain term, while quantitative research may show that users are more likely to click on a button with a certain label.

Here are some examples of how each type of research can be used:

Qualitative research in UX writing:

- **User interviews**: Conducting one-on-one interviews with users can help UX writers understand their pain points, expectations, and preferences related to language and messaging. For example, a UX writer may ask a user to describe their experience with a specific feature and take note of any language or terminology they use to describe it.

- **Usability testing:** Observing users as they interact with a product or service can reveal insights into their understanding of language and messaging. For example, a UX writer may observe users as they attempt to complete a task and listen for any confusion or hesitation related to language or terminology.

Quantitative research in UX writing:

- **A/B testing:** Running an A/B test can help UX writers determine which language or messaging resonates best with users. For example, a UX writer may test two different versions of a call-to-action button and measure which one leads to more clicks.

- **Analytics:** Tracking user behavior through analytics tools can provide insights into how users interact with language and messaging. For example, a UX writer may use analytics to determine which pages or features have the highest bounce rates, indicating a need for clearer language or messaging.

By taking a user-centered approach and using both qualitative and quantitative research methods, UX writers can create language and messaging that meets user needs and drive engagement. Let's look at an illustration of how these research methods work;

Qualitative research

A UX writer for a financial app conducts user interviews with a group of users to understand their understanding of financial jargon. Through these interviews, the writer discovers that many users are confused by terms like "APY" and "ROI". Armed with this knowledge, the UX writer revises the language used throughout the app to use simpler, more user-friendly terms.

Quantitative research

A UX writer for an e-commerce site wants to optimize the language used in their product descriptions. They run an A/B test to compare two different versions of a product description - one with more technical language and one with simpler language. After analyzing the results, they discover that the version with simpler language leads to more purchases. The UX writer then makes changes to all of the product descriptions on the site to reflect the simpler language.

Analytics

A UX writer for a news website notices that certain articles have high bounce rates, indicating that users are quickly leaving the page. Upon closer examination, the writer discovers that these articles have headlines that are misleading or confusing. Using this information, the UX writer revises the headlines to be clearer and more accurate, resulting in a decrease in bounce rates for those articles.

How to prepare User Research step-by-step

Define the research goals

Begin by defining the goals of the research. What do you want to achieve with this research? What questions do you want to answer? The research goals will guide your research design and help you choose the right methods for your study.

Choose your research method

Once you have defined your research goals, it's time to choose the research method. Some common research methods include interviews, surveys, user testing, and contextual inquiry. Each method has its own strengths and weaknesses, so choose the one that best suits your research goals.

Recruit participants

Next, you need to recruit participants for your study. Make sure your participants represent your target audience. You can recruit participants through online forums, social media, or your existing customer database.

Prepare research materials

Prepare the research materials for your study. This may include interview questions, surveys, or testing scripts. Make sure your research materials are clear and easy to understand. If you're conducting user testing, create prototypes or wireframes that reflect the user experience you want to test.

Conduct research

Conduct your research with your participants. Make sure to give clear instructions and provide support throughout the research process. Depending on your research method, you may need to record interviews or take notes during user testing.

Analyze results

Once you have completed your research, it's time to analyze the results. Look for patterns and trends in the data that can help you answer your research questions. Depending on the research method you used, you may need to transcribe interviews or code data.

Create insights

Based on your analysis, create insights that can inform your UX writing. What did you learn about your users? What do they need from your product? What pain points did you identify? These insights will help you write copy that resonates with your users.

Write copy

Finally, use your insights to write copy that meets the needs of your users. Use the language and tone that you identified in your research to make sure your copy speaks to your users. Test your copy with your users to ensure it's effective.

There are certain things that should be put into consideration before conducting user research. These things are often overlooked because it is often difficult to plan for some of these things so we often just work with them as the need arises. Some of the things to consider before research are:

1. Be intentional about the exact information that you are trying to find out from users
2. Get stakeholders involved in the research in order to get their input or suggestions before the process to avoid having to conduct the research all over again
3. Choose how to prepare or organize your results before you acquire them, in order to avoid confusion. It is helpful to create and name folders on your computer in order to easily categorize results and create order.
4. Choose the best data analysis tool that would enable you easily upload your texts, audio, or video and mark certain sections on the material to create side notes.

5. Decide on the incentives to offer the participants of your research for motivation. This may be coupons, vouchers, money, gifts, or valuable tickets. This isn't always necessary but in some cases, it would encourage more people to participate.
6. Plan the amount of time to be allocated to the research and overall budget

Now, it is time to start your research and gather all the data you can for analysis. Let's take a look at the most effective and widely used research method in UX writing;

Using Target Group Observation for research

Observation of target groups is a qualitative research method that involves observing and analyzing subjects in their natural settings, according to a definition by Channel Play. This technique goes beyond simply reading or hearing what your audience thinks or does, as it allows you to witness their behaviors under real-life circumstances. There are two main types of observation: covert and overt. In covert observation, the researcher does not reveal their identity and either blends in with the crowd or observes from a distance. Overt observation, on the other hand, involves researchers revealing themselves to the target audience or informing the subjects of their presence.

The goal of target group observation is to detect behavioral patterns and orientation patterns, gain knowledge about people's preferences, figure out which factors influence their behavior, and learn about their choice of words. It also allows for the observation of how people actually use a product. The process of target group observation involves setting research objectives, determining the questions to be asked, creating an observation guide, defining the research setting, observing as planned, gathering and analyzing data, and presenting final results to your team.

Target group observation is particularly important for UX writing because direct interviews may not provide all the necessary data. By working with observations, especially covert observation, UX writers can gain insights that their target audience may not explicitly tell them. This technique allows for a deeper understanding of the user's needs and enables writers to learn the vocabulary and terms that their audience uses when discussing a product.

The strengths of target group observation include authentic insights, no need for subject cooperation, flexibility in making changes to data, and a deeper understanding of the user's needs. However, it also has weaknesses such as being time and cost-intensive, the limited number of persons that can be observed at once, subjective data documentation, and difficulties in data consolidation and explanation of results.

When conducting target group observation, it is crucial to involve researchers early in the project, be attentive and prepared to adjust quickly, always seek permission for research, be respectful and polite towards subjects, and include a second or third observer for an unbiased opinion. By keeping these factors in mind, researchers can conduct effective target group observation and gather valuable insights for UX writing.

Competitor Analysis

Competitor analysis is an essential tool that helps UX writers to understand how other businesses are creating content and user experience. Let us take a look at the goals, how it works, why it is important in UX, its strengths, and their weaknesses.

Goals of Competitor Analysis in UX Writing

Competitor analysis in UX writing has three main goals:

Identify what your competitors are doing

UX writers can use competitor analysis to understand what their competitors are doing in terms of content and user experience. This information can help them identify areas where they can improve their content and user experience.

Analyze the effectiveness of your competitors' content

By analyzing the content of competitors, UX writers can learn what works and what does not work. This information can help them create better content and user experience.

Improve your own content and user experience

Competitor analysis in UX writing can help UX writers to identify gaps in their own content and user experience. This information can help them improve their own content and user experience to be more effective and competitive.

How Competitor Analysis in UX Writing Works

The process of competitor analysis in UX writing involves the following steps:

1. **Identify your competitors:** UX writers should start by identifying their competitors. This can be done by searching for businesses that offer similar products or services.
2. **Collect data:** The next step is to collect data on your competitors' content and user experience. This can be done by visiting their website, using their products, and analyzing their marketing materials.
3. **Analyze the data:** Once the data has been collected, UX writers can analyze it to identify trends

and patterns. This information can be used to identify areas where their competitors are strong and areas where they are weak.

4. **Use the information:** The final step is to use the information to improve their own content and user experience. UX writers can use the information to identify gaps in their own content and user experience and make improvements.

Why Competitor Analysis is Important in UX

Competitor analysis is critical in UX for several reasons:

1. Understanding the competition: Competitor analysis helps UX writers to understand their competition better. By understanding what their competitors are doing, they can identify areas where they can improve their own content and user experience.

2. Identifying gaps: Competitor analysis can help UX writers to identify gaps in their own content and user experience. By identifying these gaps, they can make improvements and create a better user experience.

3. Staying competitive: In today's business world, it is critical to stay competitive. Competitor analysis can help UX writers to identify what their competitors are doing and stay ahead of the competition.

Strengths of Competitor Analysis in UX Writing

1. **Identifying opportunities:** Competitor analysis can help UX writers to identify opportunities to improve their own content and user experience.
2. **Learning from others:** By analyzing the content and user experience of others, UX writers can learn what works and what does not work.
3. **Staying competitive:** Competitor analysis can help UX writers to stay competitive by identifying what their competitors are doing.

Weaknesses of Competitor Analysis in UX Writing

1. **It can be time-consuming:** Collecting and analyzing data on competitors can be time-consuming.
2. **It can be expensive:** Collecting data on competitors may require UX writers to purchase products or services from their competitors.
3. **It may not be accurate:** Competitor analysis may not always be accurate as the data collected may be incomplete or biased.

Conversation Mining

Conversation mining refers to the process of analyzing and extracting valuable insights from conversations between users or between users and technology. The technique is an essential part of UX writing and research, as it allows researchers to gather data on user behavior, needs, preferences, and pain points through media sources.

Sources of Conversation Mining

Conversation mining relies on various sources of data, including user feedback, customer support interactions, chat logs, social media conversations, forums, and user testing sessions. These sources engage in deep conversations about the brand and whatever opinions they may have about the products.

User Feedback: User feedback can come in various forms, including surveys, feedback forms, and reviews. Feedback helps to gather information from customers and strangers about their experience or impression of products. This is done in order to identify the gaps and disconnect between the user and the product.

Customer Support Interactions: Customer support interactions, including emails, chats, and hotline calls. They help to identify common issues and develop solutions to address them.

Chat Logs: Chat logs from messaging apps, such as Slack and WhatsApp, provide valuable data on user behavior.

Analyzing chat logs can help UX writers and researchers identify trends, patterns, and insights into user behavior.

Social Media Conversations: Social media conversations, including comments and posts, provide valuable data on user behavior, preferences, and pain points. Analyzing social media conversations can help UX writers and researchers understand how users interact with products and services and identify opportunities for improvement.

User Testing Sessions: User testing sessions provide valuable insights into user behavior and preferences. The results of user testing data can help UX writers and researchers identify areas for improvement and develop solutions to address user needs.

Goals of Conversation Mining

The primary goal of conversation mining is basically to answer the following questions:

- What do users want or need?
- What are users' pain points?
- What are the trends and patterns in user behavior?
- What opportunities exist to improve the user experience?

By answering these questions, UX writers and researchers can develop user-centric solutions that address oversight, and errors, and improve the user experience.

Process of Conversation Mining

Step 1: Data Collection: The first step in conversation mining is to collect data from various sources, including user feedback, customer support interactions, chat logs, social media conversations, and user testing sessions.

Step 2: Data Cleaning: Once the data is collected, the next step is to clean and organize it. Data cleaning involves removing duplicates, correcting errors, and formatting data for analysis.

Step 3: Data Analysis: The next step is to analyze the data to identify trends, patterns, and insights. Data analysis can be done using various techniques, including sentiment analysis, text mining, and machine learning.

Step 4: Insights and Recommendations: The final step is to identify insights and develop recommendations based on the data analysis. Insights and recommendations can be used to improve the user experience and address user needs and pain points.

Strengths of Conversation Mining

1. Provides information on what users really feel about the product.
2. Helps UX writers and researchers identify areas for improvement and develop user-centric solutions.
3. Can be used to analyze large volumes of data quickly and efficiently.

4. Can be used to identify trends and patterns in user behavior.
5. Can be used to evaluate the effectiveness of user-centric solutions.

Weaknesses of Conversation Mining

1. It relies on the quality and quantity of available data. Poor-quality data can lead to inaccurate insights and recommendations.
2. It can be challenging to analyze unstructured data, such as chat logs and social media conversations.
3. It requires specialized skills, such as data analysis and text mining.
4. It can be time-consuming and resource-intensive.

Here are some of the best tools for conversation mining:

1. **User research platforms:** Platforms such as UserTesting, UserZoom, and Userlytics can help UX writers analyze user conversations and feedback.

2. **Social media monitoring tools:** Tools such as Hootsuite, Mention, and Brand24 can enable UX writers monitor social media conversations about their brand or product.

3. **Chatbot analytics tools:** Platforms like Dialogflow and Botanalytics can aid UX writers in analyzing user

conversations with chatbots and identify areas for improvement.

4. **Customer service analytics tools:** Tools like Zendesk and Help Scout can benefit UX writers in analyzing customer support conversations and identify common issues.

5. **Voice of customer (VOC) tools:** Platforms like Qualtrics and SurveyMonkey can support UX writers in gathering feedback from customers and analyze their conversations.

6. **Natural language processing (NLP) tools:** Tools such as IBM Watson and Google Cloud Natural Language can assist UX writers to analyze and categorize user conversations based on language patterns and sentiment.

7. **Text analytics tools:** Platforms like Textio and Wordsmith can help UX writers analyze and improve their written content based on user feedback and language patterns.

8. **Conversation analysis software:** Tools such as Transana and Nvivo can enable UX writers analyze

and categorize conversations based on themes, topics, and language patterns.

Impact of Focus Groups in User Research

Focus groups are a popular qualitative research method used in UX writing. They involve bringing together a group of participants to discuss their experiences with language and text used in interfaces. Focus groups help UX writers and designers understand users' perspectives and identify areas where language can be improved to enhance user experience.

Focus groups are effective in UX writing since they allow participants to express their opinions and experiences with the language used in interfaces. Participants can discuss how they interpret language in interfaces and suggest improvements that can make it easier to use. Focus groups also allow researchers to observe how participants interact with language and text in interfaces, providing insights on how language can be improved to enhance user experience.

In addition, focus groups are cost-effective since they involve bringing together a small group of participants who share similar characteristics, reducing the cost of recruiting participants. They also provide quick results since researchers can get insights into how users interact with language and text in interfaces in a short time. Focus groups are also useful in validating assumptions made by UX writers and designers, ensuring that the language used in interfaces resonates with users.

Scenario 1: A company has developed a new mobile app for managing finances, and they want to understand how users interact with the language used in the app.

Question 1: What were your first impressions of the language used in the app?

Question 2: Do you think the language used in the app is clear and easy to understand?

Question 3: Are there any terms used in the app that you don't understand?

Question 4: Do you find the language used in the app engaging and motivating?

Scenario 2: A company has launched a new website, and they want to know how users interact with the language used in the website.

Question 1: What was your overall experience with the language used on the website?

Question 2: Did you find the language used on the website clear and easy to understand?

Question 3: Are there any terms used on the website that you don't understand?

Question 4: Do you find the language used on the website engaging and motivating?

Scenario 3: A company has developed a new chatbot for customer service, and they want to know how users interact with the language used in the chatbot.

Question 1: What were your first impressions of the language used in the chatbot?

Question 2: Did you find the language used in the chatbot clear and easy to understand?

Question 3: Were there any terms used in the chatbot that you didn't understand?

Question 4: Did you find the language used in the chatbot engaging and motivating?

Criteria for questioning focus groups

When designing focus group questions for UX writing qualitative research, there are several criteria to consider ensuring the questions are effective in eliciting insightful responses from participants. Here are some of the key criteria:

1. **Open-ended questions:** Focus group questions should be open-ended, allowing participants to share their thoughts and opinions freely without being

constrained by predefined answer options. This helps to elicit more detailed and nuanced responses.

2. **Relevant to the research goals**: The questions should be designed to address the research objectives and provide insights into the user experience, product usage, or other key factors being investigated.

3. **Clear and concise:** The questions should be easy to understand and concise, avoiding technical jargon or confusing language that could confuse participants.

4. **Non-leading:** Questions should be phrased in a neutral way, avoiding leading language or assumptions that could bias participants' responses.

5. **Inclusive:** Questions should be inclusive and avoid assumptions about participants' age, gender, race, or other personal characteristics. This helps to ensure that the focus group is welcoming and accessible to all participants.

6. **Varied:** Focus group questions should cover a range of topics and perspectives to provide a comprehensive understanding of the user experience.

7. **Sequenced:** Questions should be sequenced in a logical order that builds upon earlier questions and helps participants to gradually explore and articulate their thoughts and feelings.

Pros of focus group questioning in UX writing qualitative research:

1. Diversity of opinions: Focus groups bring together a diverse group of individuals who can offer a range of opinions and perspectives on a particular topic. This can help UX writers gain a deeper understanding of user needs and preferences.
2. Real-time feedback: Focus groups allow UX writers to receive real-time feedback on their content, which can help them identify any issues or areas for improvement.
3. Group dynamics: Focus groups can foster group dynamics that lead to more in-depth and nuanced discussions. Participants can build on each other's ideas and insights, which can result in richer data.
4. Cost-effective: Focus groups can be a cost-effective way to conduct research, as it allows UX writers to gather data from multiple participants at once.

Cons of focus group questioning in UX writing qualitative research:

1. Groupthink: Group dynamics can also lead to groupthink, where participants may conform to the opinions of others rather than express their own views. This can result in biased data and limit the usefulness of the research.
2. Limited sample size: Focus groups typically involve a small sample size, which can limit the generalizability

of the findings. It may be necessary to conduct multiple focus groups to gather sufficient data.

3. Difficulty in recruiting participants: Recruiting participants for focus groups can be challenging, especially if the target user group is small or difficult to reach.

4. Difficulty in analyzing data: Analyzing data from focus groups can be time-consuming and requires skilled researchers who can identify patterns and themes in the data.

Chapter 6

The Role of Validating User Research

Evaluative research is often referred to as validating user research. This research methodology aims to test the effectiveness and clarity of a copy by analyzing and collecting data from users. It is used to validate hypotheses and concepts related to interface functions of websites, mobile apps, applications, and services. Some of the methods used in validating user research include search team analysis, A/B testing, card sorting, comprehensive surveys, close testing, usability tests, highlighter testing, and others.

The two forms of user research are exploratory research and validating research. Exploratory research involves examining subjects in an attempt to gain further insights before building a product feature. On the other hand, validating research involves collecting and analyzing data to test and validate certain hypotheses and concepts.

To prepare for validating user research, one should be aware of what they want to find out by looking at three different sources, namely, company KPIs, UX writing quality criteria, and general content criteria. The criteria for UX writing quality include the text being necessary, concise, clear, useful, conversational, and branded. The fundamental categories of content criteria include readability, usability, comprehension, navigability, accessibility, and searchability.

It is essential to define the purpose of the copy element to be tested to determine if it fulfills its intended purpose. The results of the research should be prepared and organized in a structured manner, and the researcher should educate themselves about various user research methods. Additionally, data privacy rules and laws should be considered when conducting exploratory research.

Validating user research is critical for UX writing since it helps ensure the quality of the copy, shows the impact of writing decisions to stakeholders, and provides clarity on how to improve the copy. It also allows one to understand how users perceive their voice and tone, learn about the target audience, improve writing skills, and identify personal biases. Let's look at some approaches to validating user research.

Utilizing Search Term Analysis

Search term analysis is a powerful tool that can help UX writers make informed decisions when choosing the best language to use for their copy. It involves analyzing search terms to determine their popularity, comparative power, and changes in usage over time. By using data to inform language choices, UX writers can improve the user experience and increase the chances of their content ranking well in search engine results.

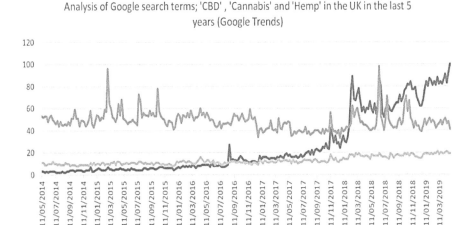

Analysis of Google search terms; 'CBD' , 'Cannabis' and 'Hemp' in the UK in the last 5 years (Google Trends)

Search term analysis has evolved significantly over time, from simply tracking the most popular search terms on search engines to utilizing advanced analytics tools to gather insights about user behavior and preferences.

Initially, search term analysis involved identifying the most commonly searched terms and using them to inform website content and optimization strategies. This approach was relatively simplistic and didn't provide a deep understanding of user intent or behavior.

However, with the advent of more advanced analytics tools, search term analysis has become much more sophisticated. Today, UX writers and researchers can use tools like Google Analytics and SEMrush to analyze search terms, user behavior, and preferences. These tools allow them to track user behavior, monitor search trends, and gain insights into user intent and preferences.

To conduct a search term analysis, it is important to set research objectives and define the concepts for which terminology is needed. Once the objectives are clear, the preferred tool and platform can be chosen. There are various tools available for conducting search term analysis, such as Google Trends, Ahrefs, SEMrush, and Moz.

Let's take for example, a UX writer who is working on a project to write copy for a landing page of a startup that provides online courses. The writer needs to understand which term to use, such as "online course," "e-learning," or "virtual learning." By analyzing data on how often each term is used by people, the UX writer can make an informed decision on the best terminology to use for the landing page.

One of the strengths of search term analysis is that it provides extensive data material for reliable insights, which can be easily accessed and analyzed. The results are also easy to communicate to other stakeholders. However, it is important to keep in mind the weaknesses of this method, such as the potential for inaccurate results if the input is not correct and the non-transparent reliability of data.

To overcome these weaknesses, it is important to use interchangeable terms for comparison, adjust the settings to the specific target market, and validate the results using different tools. In addition, it is important to get familiar with the functioning logic of the tools used for search term analysis.

By using data to inform language choices, UX writers can create better user experiences and improve SEO ranking. By keeping in mind the strengths and weaknesses of this method and following the recommended best practices, UX writers can make the most out of search term analysis and improve the effectiveness of their writing.

Furthermore, search term analysis is not only useful for native English speakers but also for non-native speakers who may struggle with choosing the right word or phrase to use in their writing. Data-based decisions can help eliminate language barriers and ensure clarity for all users.

It is important to note that search term analysis should not be the only factor in decision-making for UX writing. Popularity does not always equate to the appropriateness, and context must always be considered. Other factors such as tone, voice, and messaging must also be taken into account when crafting effective UX copy.

A/B Testing in User Research

A/B testing, also known as split testing, is a method of comparing two versions of a product or content to see which one performs better. This can be used for a wide range of elements in user experience, including copy, design, functionality, and more. By using A/B testing, UX writers can make data-driven decisions about what works best for their users.

Here's everything you need to know about A/B testing as a UX writer. This includes how to plan and execute a test, how to interpret the results, and how to use them to improve your content.

Planning an A/B Test

Before you begin an A/B test, you need to have a clear goal in mind. This could be anything from increasing click-through rates on a call-to-action button to improving engagement with a specific piece of content. Once you have a goal, you can begin to plan your test.

First, identify the element you want to test. This could be a headline, a button, a form field, or any other element of your product or content. Make sure you only test one element at a time, otherwise, you won't be able to determine which change caused the difference in performance.

Next, create two versions of the element you want to test. One version will be the control, or the original version, and the other will be the variant, or the version with the change you want to test. The control and the variant should be identical except for the one element you are testing.

Determine how long you want to run the test. This will depend on the amount of traffic your site or product receives, as well as the size of the difference you expect to see. In general, a test should run for at least a week to ensure you have enough data to make an informed decision.

Executing an A/B Test

Once you have a plan in place, it's time to execute your A/B test. There are a few things to keep in mind when running a test to ensure that your results are accurate and reliable.

First, make sure that your test is running on a large enough sample size. If you have too few users participating in the test, the results may not be statistically significant. A good rule of thumb is to aim for at least 100 participants per variant.

Second, make sure that your test is randomizing the traffic between the control and the variant. This will ensure that any differences in performance are not due to external factors, such as time of day or day of the week.

In order to proceed, you need to sign up.

Please create an Account

Already have an account? Log in.

Create an account to enjoy all the benefits of UX writing INC.

We'd love to have you onboard.

Already have an account? Log in.

Make sure that you are tracking the right metrics. Depending on your goal, this could be anything from click-through rates to bounce rates to time on the page. Choose a metric that directly measures the success of your goal.

Interpreting A/B Test Results

Once your test is complete, it's time to interpret the results. There are a few different metrics you'll want to look at to determine which variant performed better.

The first metric to look at is statistical significance. This tells you whether the difference in performance between the control and the variant is due to chance or if it's a real difference. In general, you want a statistical significance of at least 95% to be confident in your results.

Next, look at the actual performance metrics. Did the variant perform better than the control? If so, by how much? Make sure to look at both the absolute and relative differences in performance.

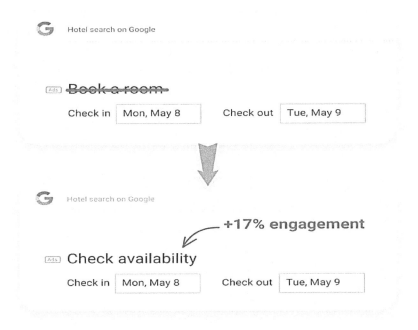

Look at any potential side effects of the change. Did the change have any unintended consequences? For example, did changing the color of a button increase click-through rates but decrease engagement with the rest of the page?

Using A/B Test Results to Improve Content

Once you've interpreted the results of your A/B test, it's time to use them to improve your content. Here are a few tips for doing so effectively:

1. Implement the winning variant: If the variant performed better than the control, implement the change on your site or product. This will help you improve the user experience and achieve your goal.
2. Iterate and test again: A/B testing is an iterative process. Once you've implemented the winning variant, test another change to see if you can continue to improve performance.
3. Share your results: A/B testing can be a collaborative process. Share your results with other stakeholders in the product or content to get their feedback and insights.
4. Keep testing: A/B testing should be an ongoing process. Continuously test and iterate to improve the user experience and achieve your goals.

Here are a few illustrations of how A/B testing can be used in UX writing:

Example 1: Testing a Call-to-Action Button

Goal: Increase click-through rates on a call-to-action button.

Element to test: The color of the call-to-action button.

Control: A blue button that says "Sign up now."

Variant: A green button that says "Sign up now."

Results: The green button increased click-through rates by 20%, with a statistical significance of 99%.

Action: Implement the green button on the site.

Example 2: Testing a Headline

Goal: Increase engagement with a blog post.

Element to test: The headline of the blog post.

Control: "10 Tips for Better UX Writing."

Variant: "10 Secrets to Writing Better UX Copy."

Results: The variant increased time on page by 15%, with a statistical significance of 97%.

Action: Implement the variant headline on the blog post.

Example 3: Testing a Form Field Label

Goal: Increase form completion rates.

Element to test: The label of a form field.

Control: "Email Address."

Variant: "Your Email."

Results: The variant increased form completion rates by 10%, with a statistical significance of 95%.

Action: Implement the variant form field label on the form.

CTA BUTTON COLOR

Version A

Hi!

We've just launched a new feature - Email Scheduling.

Now you can:
- schedule according to the recipient's time zone
- choose the days on which no emails will be sent
- set hours between which emails will be delivered for maximum engagement
- plus, set up follow-up reminders

Hope you enjoy it!
Test out the new feature by clicking the button below.

TRY NOW

Version B

Hi!

We've just launched a new feature - Email Scheduling.

Now you can:
- schedule according to the recipient's time zone
- choose the days on which no emails will be sent
- set hours between which emails will be delivered for maximum engagement
- plus, set up follow-up reminders

Hope you enjoy it!
Test out the new feature by clicking the button below.

TRY NOW

Click-through rate results

38% vs 25%

Version A | Version B

As you can see, A/B testing can provide valuable insights into how users interact with your content, and it can help you make data-driven decisions about how to improve the user experience. However, it's important to keep in mind that A/B testing is just one tool in the UX writer's toolkit. It should be used in combination with other research methods, such as user testing and surveys, to gain a holistic understanding of user needs and behavior.

When conducting A/B tests, it's also important to keep in mind ethical considerations. For example, you should ensure that tests are designed in a way that does not harm users or mislead them. You should also be transparent about the fact that users are participating in a test and provide them with the option to opt-out if they choose to do so.

In addition, it's important to have a solid understanding of statistical analysis and significance testing when interpreting the results of an A/B test. This will help you avoid common pitfalls, such as mistaking random noise for a significant difference between variants.

A/B testing is a powerful tool for UX writers looking to improve the user experience and achieve their goals. By following best practices and being mindful of ethical considerations, UX writers can use A/B testing to make data-driven decisions that lead to better user experiences.

Understanding Comprehension Surveys in User Research

Comprehension surveys are an important tool that UX writers can use to test their copy's clarity and effectiveness. They help to identify misunderstandings and ambiguities, improve writing skills, and see which parts of the copy need further improvement. Many companies use comprehensive surveys in various capacities and they are used both online and offline.

What are Comprehension Surveys?

Comprehension surveys are questionnaires that test a user's understanding of a piece of content. They can range from short strings to long pieces, and everything in between. The objective of a comprehension survey is to provide quick questions to users to test their understanding of a feature or piece of content. For example, a target audience can be shown a feature inside an app or website, and then asked what they think the feature does. The participants can then choose from a list of options, including an open-answer option to elaborate on their choices.

How do Comprehension Surveys Work?

The methodology isn't very different from other forms of survey. To conduct a comprehension survey, the following steps are needed:

- **Create an objective for your research:** Determine which part of your copy you want to test.
- **Determine the scope:** Decide on the sample size and the metrics you will use to measure your results.
- **Develop your questions:** Select a survey tool and develop questions that align with your research objectives.
- **Recruit people for your survey:** Recruit participants who match your target audience and run your survey.
- **Analyze collected data:** Collect and analyze the data from your survey.

- **Make decisions from your results:** Present your results to stakeholders and discuss decisions based on the data.

Why are Comprehension Surveys so important for UX Writing?

Comprehension surveys are literally the voice of the people. They are critical to UX writing as they delve into the depths of how quickly and easily our texts can be understood by users. if we create products with the assumption that users understand their meanings or how to navigate through certain areas then we would have failed in the design phase. By providing a platform for participants to choose from different options, UX writers gain insights into why certain copy might be difficult to comprehend at certain points. Conducting comprehension surveys on a larger scale with a tool like Google Forms allows UX writers to gather vast amounts of data, which can be analyzed and used to improve their copy.

Comprehension surveys have several advantages and disadvantages that some are not aware of. By conducting surveys, it is assumed that the biggest challenge is getting people to actually participate in the survey, but there's more to it than meets the eye. Let's take a closer look.

Advantages

- Comprehension surveys provide clear and easy-to-understand insights on the copy's effectiveness.
- They are low cost, and many text elements can be tested at once.
- The data is easy to analyze, and results are easy to communicate.

Disadvantages

- They only reveal which copy is better, but not the "why" behind it. it would have been better if the ux writer was also able to find out the "Why" before accepting the results.
- The cooperation of participants is required, which can be challenging to obtain.
- It can be difficult to recruit enough participants as people often want incentives befrore they are motivated to participate.
- Context is often lacking and can affect the quality of the result.

When conducting comprehension surveys, several things need to be kept in mind:

- Focus on the basic UX writing quality criteria.
- Test for crossability, voice, and time.
- Ensure that questions are largely open-answer to gain additional information.

Here is an sample of what a comprehension survey looks like:

1. How did you first hear about our ecommerce app?
2. What is the primary reason you use our ecommerce app?
3. How frequently do you use our ecommerce app?
4. What are the main features you use on our ecommerce app?
5. How easy was it to find the product you were looking for?
6. Did you find the search function useful? Why or why not?
7. Were you able to easily navigate through the app to find what you were looking for?
8. Did you encounter any issues while navigating through the app? If yes, please specify.
9. Did you find the product information and details helpful?
10. Were you able to easily compare products on our ecommerce app?
11. Were you satisfied with the checkout process? If not, please specify any issues you faced.
12. How likely are you to recommend our ecommerce app to a friend or colleague?
13. Do you have any suggestions for improving our ecommerce app?

Tabulated Survey Results:

Survey Question	Strongly Disagree	Disagree	Neutral	Agree	Strongly Agree
How easy was it to find the product you were looking for?					
Did you find the search function useful? Why or why not?					
Were you able to easily navigate through the app to find what you were looking for?					
Did you encounter any issues					

Survey Question	Strongly Disagree	Disagree	Neutral	Agree	Strongly Agree
while navigating through the app? If yes, please specify.					
Did you find the product information and details helpful?					
Were you able to easily compare products on our ecommerce app?					
Were you satisfied with the checkout process? If not, please specify any					

Survey Question	Strongly Disagree	Disagree	Neutral	Agree	Strongly Agree
issues you faced.					
How likely are you to recommend our ecommerce app to a friend or colleague?					
Do you have any suggestions for improving our ecommerce app?					

Developing Information Architecture with Card Sorting

Card sorting is a method used in user research to understand how users organize and categorize information. It involves sorting a set of cards that contain various items into groups or categories that make sense to the user.

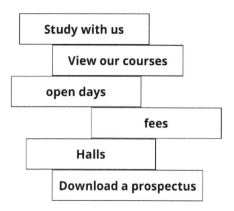

The goal of card sorting is to gather insights into how users think about and organize information, which can inform the design of user interfaces, website navigation, and information architecture. Through it, we learn user expectations towards conventions.

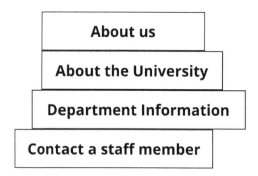

There are three types of card sorting: open, closed, and hybrid.

Open Card Sorting:

In open card sorting, participants are given a set of cards without any predefined categories. They are asked to sort the cards into groups and create their own categories. This approach allows researchers to gather insights into how users think about and group information, without any influence from pre-existing categories.

Closed Card Sorting:

In this card sorting, participants are given a set of cards with pre-defined categories. They are asked to sort the cards into these pre-existing categories. This approach is useful when a researcher wants to validate an existing information architecture or test the effectiveness of a current navigation system.

Hybrid Card Sorting:

In this method, the participants can either sort the cards into pre-existing categories or they may change the categories themselves.

Here is an illustration of how card sorting works: let's say that you are asked to write a copy for a company and you are uncertain of how your copy sounds to users. What you can do is write the same copy in various versions and then write down a set of values such as:

- Fun
- Bold
- Cool
- Innovative

Next, ask an audience to sort your copies into which category they feel describes the tone of your copy. Here's what it would probably look like:

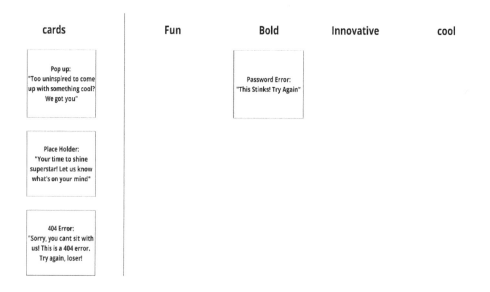

The open, closed, and hybrid card sorting have their benefits and can be used in different situations. Below are some key benefits of card sorting in User research:

1. Understanding user mental models: Card sorting helps UX designers to understand how users group and categorize information in their minds. This understanding can be used to develop user interfaces that align with users' mental models and make it easier for them to find the information they need.
2. Validating information architecture: Card sorting can be used to validate an existing information architecture. This approach can help UX designers to identify any gaps or inconsistencies in the information architecture and make necessary adjustments.
3. Improving website navigation: Card sorting can be used to optimize website navigation by helping UX designers to identify the most logical and intuitive categories for grouping information.
4. Saving time and resources: Card sorting can help UX designers to gather valuable insights from users before investing time and resources into building a website or application. This approach can help to minimize the risk of designing an ineffective user interface.

When conducting card sorting, there are several best practices that UX designers should follow:

1. Recruit participants who represent the target audience.

2. Use a sufficient number of cards to cover the range of information that needs to be sorted.
3. Ensure that the cards are easy to read and understand.
4. Provide clear instructions and explain the purpose of the activity.
5. Use an online tool or software to streamline the process and ensure accurate data collection.

Here are some great tools that can help with sorting information in user research:

Card sorting is a valuable method for UX designers to gain insight into how users organize and categorize information. By understanding users' mental models and information organization preferences, UX designers can create user interfaces that are intuitive, efficient, and easy to use.

USABILITY TESTING in User Research

Usability testing is another overlooked aspect of the user experience design process. Like every other design, it typically involves evaluating how users interact with a product or website to identify areas of improvement. Let's take a look at what makes it so special.

Defining Usability Testing

Usability testing is a qualitative research method in which a moderator asks a participant to complete a task and then asks them questions about their experience. This method allows designers to gain insight into how users interact with a product or website and identify areas that need improvement. Usability testing typically involves providing users with a prototype or a live product or website and asking them to complete a certain task with it. During the test, the moderator asks the participant to describe their thoughts and experiences, and provides an opportunity for the participant to give feedback on what works well and what doesn't.

The Goal of Usability Testing

The goal of usability testing is to identify usability problems and misunderstandings that users may encounter while using a product or website. This information can then be used to improve the overall user experience. Usability testing is particularly useful for UX writers, as it allows them to test the overall flow of their copy, not just individual pieces of text. Through usability testing, UX writers can learn how their copy helps users solve a problem, as well as identify any misunderstandings or ambiguity that may be present.

How Usability Testing Works

The process of usability testing involves several steps. First, researchers must set their research objective and scope of testing. They must then prepare their test guide, choose a suitable tool and build a prototype. Once the prototype is ready, researchers must define their sample audience and plan the procedure for the study. This includes determining the target audience, how many people to invite, how much time to spend conducting the test, and what kind of incentives to offer your participants in order to motivate them. The actual usability test is then conducted, and the data is prepared and analyzed. Finally, the results are presented to the team and discussed to make decisions on how to improve the product or website.

Here's an example of Usability Testing in action

Let's say you are a UX writer for an ecommerce shop that allows customers to customize a designer shoe and then purchase it. Your task is to write copy for the customization and purchase flow, which involves choosing the size, color, details, and payment information. To ensure that your copy makes sense and the flow is smooth, you can conduct a usability test. Invite users to the website and ask them to customize a sneaker, providing demo payment details and allowing them to "buy" the shoe virtually. Through this process, you can identify any usability problems and make improvements to your copy.

The Importance of Usability Testing for UX Writing

Usability testing is essential for testing the overall concept of UX writing decisions. It enables UX writers to test all aspects of their copy in context, rather than testing individual pieces of text. This method is also valuable for identifying flows that need improvement and making changes to copy at any phase of the process. When conducting usability testing, it's important to choose participants that represent the diversity of the target audience.

Advantages and Disadvantages of Usability Testing

Like any research method, usability testing has both pros and cons. Some of the advantages of usability testing include evaluating copy in the context of a flow, testing several text elements at once, and gaining insight into user expectations, language, habits, motives, and needs. However, usability testing can also consume significant time and money, and it's often only feasible to test a small sample of users. Additionally, it requires strong research skills to analyze the data, and subject cooperation is crucial.

When conducting usability tests, there are several things to keep in mind. First, it's important to carefully choose participants because choosing people outside your target demographic will always yield poor results.

Illustration of Usability Test

TEST 1 - Website: Amazon.com

Task: Sign up for a new Amazon account

Goal: Evaluate the ease of creating a new Amazon account and completing the sign-up process.

Pre-task questions:

a. Have you used Amazon before?

b. Do you have an existing Amazon account?

c. Have you signed up for a new account on any other websites recently?

Task steps:

a. Go to the Amazon homepage.

b. Click on "Account & Lists" in the top right corner of the page.

c. Click on "Start here" under the "New customer?" heading.

d. Enter your name, email address, and desired password.

e. Click on "Create your Amazon account."

f. Enter your billing and shipping information.

g. Review your information and click on "Create your Amazon account" again.

h. Check your email for a verification code from Amazon.

i. Enter the code on the Amazon website to complete the sign-up process.

Post-task questions:

a. Did you encounter any issues while signing up for a new Amazon account?

b. Was the sign-up process easy to complete?

c. Was the information requested during sign-up clear and understandable?

d. Were there any steps in the process that you found confusing or unnecessary?

e. On a scale of 1 to 10, how likely are you to recommend Amazon to a friend based on this sign-up experience?

TEST 2 - Booking a Vacation Rental on Airbnb.com

Objective: To test the ease and effectiveness of the flow for booking a vacation rental on Airbnb's website.

Steps:

1. Navigate to Airbnb.com and search for a vacation rental of your choice.
2. Filter the search results to match your preferences (e.g., dates, number of guests, amenities).
3. Click on the desired rental to open its listing page.
4. Review the rental information, including its location, amenities, house rules, and cancellation policy.
5. Check the availability of the rental for your desired dates.
6. Click on the "Request to Book" button located on the right-hand side of the page.

7. Enter your travel details, including your check-in and check-out dates, the number of guests, and any additional requirements or questions for the host.
8. Review the total price, including any fees or taxes.
9. Click on the "Request to Book" button to send your booking request to the host.

Success Criteria:

- The user should be able to easily find the desired vacation rental and access its listing page.
- The search filters should be easily accessible and effective in narrowing down the search results.
- The rental information should be comprehensive and include all necessary details.
- The availability calendar should be up-to-date and accurate.
- The "Request to Book" button should be prominently displayed and easily clickable.
- The booking process should be straightforward and easy to follow.

Metrics to Measure:

- Time taken to complete the task
- Number of clicks required to book the rental
- User satisfaction ratings for the flow

Potential Issues to Monitor:

- Difficulty in finding the desired vacation rental or accessing its listing page.

- Issues with the search filters, such as not working as intended or not displaying the correct results.
- Missing or incomplete rental information that may cause confusion or hesitation for the user.
- Issues with the availability calendar not being accurate or up-to-date.
- Issues with the "Request to Book" button, such as it being difficult to click or not functioning properly.
- Issues with the booking process, such as confusing or unclear steps or errors during the submission of the booking request.

There are several great tools available for conducting usability tests in UX writing. Here are some of them:

1. UsabilityHub: UsabilityHub offers a suite of tools for conducting quick and easy usability tests, including the Five Second Test, Click Test, Question Test, and Navigation Test. These tests allow you to get quick feedback on various aspects of your design and writing. https://usabilityhub.com/

2. UserTesting: UserTesting offers a platform for conducting remote usability tests with participants from around the world. You can test various aspects of your UX, including writing, design, and functionality, and get feedback from real users. https://www.usertesting.com/

3. Optimal Workshop: Optimal Workshop offers a suite of tools for conducting user research and testing, including Treejack, OptimalSort, and Chalkmark. These tools allow you to test the usability of your information architecture, navigation, and user flows. https://www.optimalworkshop.com/

4. Hotjar: Hotjar is a tool that allows you to track user behavior on your website or app, including how users interact with your UX writing. You can use this data to optimize your writing and design for better usability. https://www.hotjar.com/

5. UserZoom: UserZoom offers a suite of tools for conducting remote user research and testing, including usability testing, card sorting, and surveys. These tools allow you to get feedback from real users on various aspects of your UX. https://www.userzoom.com/

Cloze Testing in User Research

Cloze testing is a language assessment technique that originated in the field of linguistics. It was first introduced by Wilson Taylor in 1953, and since then, it has become a popular tool for testing language proficiency. Cloze testing is now widely used in education, marketing, and user experience (UX) writing to evaluate language comprehension and to improve the overall user experience.

Definition of Cloze Testing

Cloze testing is a language assessment technique that involves removing words from a text and asking the reader to fill in the blanks with appropriate words. The missing words can be any part of speech, including nouns, verbs, adjectives, and adverbs. The purpose of cloze testing is to evaluate the reader's ability to comprehend the text and to use context clues to fill in the blanks.

Types of Cloze Tests

There are two main types of cloze tests: open and closed. An open cloze test requires the reader to fill in the blanks with any word that makes sense in the context of the sentence. In contrast, a closed cloze test provides a list of options for the reader to choose from when filling in the blanks.

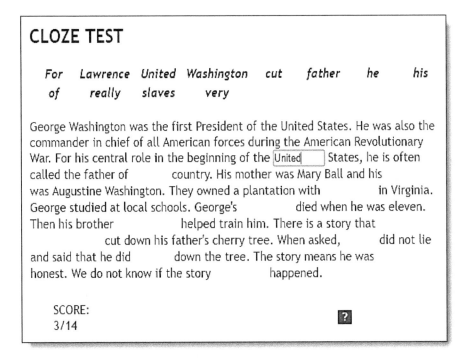

CLOZE TEST

For   Lawrence   United   Washington   cut   father   he   his
of   really   slaves   very

George Washington was the first President of the United States. He was also the commander in chief of all American forces during the American Revolutionary War. For his central role in the beginning of the [United   ] States, he is often called the father of   country. His mother was Mary Ball and his   was Augustine Washington. They owned a plantation with   in Virginia. George studied at local schools. George's   died when he was eleven. Then his brother   helped train him. There is a story that   cut down his father's cherry tree. When asked,   did not lie and said that he did   down the tree. The story means he was   honest. We do not know if the story   happened.

SCORE:
3/14

Another type of cloze test is the modified cloze test, which involves removing only certain types of words from the text, such as prepositions or conjunctions. The modified cloze test is often used to evaluate specific language skills, such as grammar or vocabulary.

The Practice of Cloze Testing

Cloze testing is commonly used in UX writing to evaluate the readability and comprehension of text. UX writers use cloze testing to test the effectiveness of their language, to identify areas where users may struggle to understand the text, and to improve the overall user experience.

To conduct a cloze test, UX writers begin by selecting a piece of text that they want to evaluate. The text can be any type of content, such as an email, a landing page, or an instruction manual. Once the text has been selected, the UX writer removes every nth word from the text, where n is typically between 4 and 6. The missing words are then replaced with a blank space, and the text is presented to a group of test participants.

The test participants are asked to fill in the blanks with the word that they believe best fits the context of the sentence. The UX writer then evaluates the responses to determine whether the test participants understood the text and whether the language was effective in conveying the intended message.

Importance of Cloze Testing in UX Writing

Cloze testing is an essential tool for UX writers because it helps to identify areas where users may struggle to understand the text. By evaluating user responses to cloze tests, UX writers can gain insight into the effectiveness of their language, and they can make changes to improve the overall user experience.

Cloze testing can also help UX writers to identify potential usability issues. For example, if test participants consistently provide incorrect responses to certain blanks in the text, it may indicate that the language is unclear or that the user interface is confusing.

Moreover, cloze testing helps UX writers to create content that is more engaging and user-friendly. By identifying areas where users may struggle to understand the text, UX writers can make changes to the language to make it more accessible and understandable.

Limitations of Cloze Testing

While cloze testing is a valuable tool for evaluating language comprehension and improving the user experience, it does have its limitations. One limitation of cloze testing is that it may not accurately reflect real-world language use. In the real world, people rarely encounter text with random words removed, and they are often able to use context clues to infer the meaning of unfamiliar words.

Another limitation of cloze testing is that it may be biased towards certain types of language skills, such as vocabulary or grammar. For example, a test that removes only prepositions may be biased towards evaluating the knowledge of prepositions rather than overall language comprehension.

Cloze testing may also be affected by factors such as cultural background and language proficiency. Test participants may have different levels of familiarity with certain types of vocabulary or syntax, depending on their cultural background or first language. This can affect their ability to accurately fill in the blanks and may result in skewed test results.

Despite these limitations, cloze testing remains a valuable tool for UX writers to evaluate language comprehension and improve the overall user experience. By combining cloze testing with other methods of language assessment, such as usability testing and user surveys, UX writers can gain a comprehensive understanding of how users interact with their content and make informed decisions about how to improve it.

Best Practices for Cloze Testing in UX Writing

To get the most accurate and useful results from cloze testing, UX writers should follow best practices for designing and conducting tests. These best practices include:

1. Selecting appropriate text: The text selected for cloze testing should be representative of the content that users will encounter in the product or service. It should also be of an appropriate length, typically between 50 and 100 words, to ensure that participants can complete the test quickly and accurately.
2. Using a diverse participant pool: To ensure that the results of the cloze test are representative of the user population, UX writers should recruit a diverse pool of test participants. This can include participants of different ages, genders, cultural backgrounds, and language proficiencies.

3. Randomizing blank selection: To avoid bias in the results, UX writers should randomly select the words to remove from the text. This ensures that each test participant encounters a different set of blanks, reducing the likelihood of shared answers.
4. Providing clear instructions: UX writers should provide clear instructions to test participants, including how to fill in the blanks and any time limits for completing the test. Clear instructions help to ensure that test results are accurate and reliable.
5. Analyzing results carefully: UX writers should carefully analyze the results of the cloze test to identify patterns and trends in the data. This can help to identify areas where users may struggle to understand the language and inform changes to improve the overall user experience.

Open Cloze Testing Example:

Text: The world of business is constantly changing, and companies must adapt to stay competitive. One way businesses can adapt is by embracing new technologies, such as artificial intelligence and machine learning. These technologies can help businesses automate processes, analyze data more efficiently, and make better decisions.

Another way businesses can stay competitive is by fostering a culture of _____. This means encouraging employees to take risks, share ideas, and think creatively. When employees feel empowered to experiment and innovate, they are more likely to come up with new products and services that can drive the company's growth.

Blank 1: Businesses can adapt by embracing new _____ such as artificial intelligence and machine learning.

Blank 2: Another way businesses can stay competitive is by fostering a culture of _____.

Answer 1: technologies

Answer 2: innovation

Closed Cloze Testing Example:

Text: The ancient civilization of Egypt is known for its impressive architecture, art, and engineering. The pyramids of Giza, for example, are some of the most iconic structures in the world, and the Sphinx is a marvel of ancient engineering. Egyptian art is also highly regarded for its beauty and detail, with hieroglyphics serving as a written language that helped to preserve their culture.

Egyptian society was highly structured, with a rigid social hierarchy that placed the pharaoh at the top. The pharaoh was considered a god king, and his rule was absolute.

Beneath him were the nobles, priests, and scribes, followed by the farmers and laborers.

Blank 1: The _____ of Giza are some of the most iconic structures in the world.

Blank 2: Egyptian _____ is highly regarded for its beauty and detail.

Blank 3: The _____ was considered a god-king, and his rule was absolute.

Options: a) Sphinx b) pyramids c) art d) pharaoh e) architecture f) social hierarchy

Answer 1: b) pyramids

Answer 2: c) art

Answer 3: d) pharaoh

Here are some of the best tools for cloze testing:

1. Google Forms: https://www.google.com/forms/about/
2. SurveyMonkey: https://www.surveymonkey.com/
3. Typeform: https://www.typeform.com/
4. UserTesting: https://www.usertesting.com/
5. Hotjar: https://www.hotjar.com/
6. Clozeit: https://clozeit.syedkhairi.com/

Highlighter Testing in UX Writing

Highlighter Testing, also known as sentence highlighting or sentence testing, has been around for decades. The method was initially developed in the 1950s and 1960s by researchers in the field of linguistics who were interested in studying sentence structure and syntax. Later, usability experts adapted this testing method to evaluate the clarity of text used in user interfaces, such as websites and mobile applications.

What is Highlighter Testing?

Highlighter testing is a qualitative method of evaluating the clarity and effectiveness of text by asking users to highlight or underline words or phrases that they find confusing or difficult to understand. The method can be used to test any type of text, including instructional materials, marketing copy, and product descriptions.

Most banks require Two-factor authentication to log in with a new device. Typically, users will add their email address and phone number for this process. You will proceed automatically in order to reach the dashboard after you approve your Log In request. In some cases, users will receive a physical device to authenticate themselves.

Types of Highlighter Testing

There are two types of highlighter testing: remote and in-person. Remote highlighter testing is conducted online, while in-person highlighter testing is conducted in a physical location.

Remote Highlighter Testing: In remote highlighter testing, users are provided with a digital copy of the text to be tested and are asked to highlight or underline the words or phrases that they find confusing or difficult to understand. This method is typically conducted using a remote user testing platform or an online survey tool.

In-Person Highlighter Testing: In-person highlighter testing is conducted in a physical location, such as a usability lab or focus group facility. Users are provided with a printed copy of the text to be tested and are asked to highlight or underline the words or phrases that they find confusing or difficult to understand.

How Does It Work?

To conduct a highlighter test, follow these steps:

Step 1: The first step is to develop the text to be tested. This may include product descriptions, instructional materials, marketing copy, or any other type of text that will be used in the product.

Step 2: Choose the participants who will be taking part in the highlighter test. Participants should represent the target audience for the product and should have little or no prior knowledge of the product.

Step 3: The test can be conducted remotely or in person. Participants are provided with a copy of the text to be tested and are asked to highlight or underline any words or phrases that they find confusing or difficult to understand. They may also be asked to provide feedback on the text, such as suggestions for improving clarity or wording.

Step 4: After the test is complete, analyze the results to identify patterns in the areas of the text that participants found confusing or difficult to understand. Use this information to revise the text as needed to improve clarity and effectiveness.

How is Highlighter Testing Used?

1. **Testing Text Highlighting for Readability:** When designing an interface with large amounts of text, a UX writer may use highlighter testing to determine which phrases or sections of text are most important or difficult to understand. For example, a UX writer may test the use of yellow highlighting to draw attention to key phrases, and blue highlighting to emphasize important terms. They may also test the use of different colors or styles of highlighting to distinguish between different types of information. The purpose of this type of highlighter testing is to improve the readability and user experience of the text.

2. **Testing Highlighted Links for Visibility:** When designing an interface with hyperlinks, a UX writer may use highlighter testing to determine which colors or styles of highlighting make the links most visible and clickable. For example, a UX writer may test the use of bright red highlighting for links to important pages, and underlining for links to related content. They may also test the use of different colors or styles of highlighting to distinguish between different types of links. The purpose of this type of highlighter testing is to improve the user's ability to navigate and interact with the interface.

Limitations of the highlighter test

While highlighter testing is a useful tool for evaluating the clarity of text, it does have limitations. For example, the method may not capture more nuanced issues, such as tone and voice, which can also impact the effectiveness of the text. Additionally, participants may not always be able to articulate why they found certain words or phrases confusing or difficult to understand.

Highlighting content

In this activity, mark words or phrases like this:

I can understand this

I am confused by this

There are several tools available for assessing and improving readability in UX writing. Here are a few popular ones:

1. **Hemingway Editor:** This tool analyzes your text and provides suggestions to simplify and clarify your writing. It highlights complex sentences, passive voice, adverbs, and other areas for improvement.

1 adverb, meeting the goal of 7 or fewer.

0 uses of passive voice. Nice work.

0 phrases have simpler alternatives.

1 of 34 sentences is hard to read.

2 of 34 sentences are very hard to read.

Hemingway *Editor*

Readability

Grade 4
Good

Reading time: **00:01:15**
Letters: **1425**
Characters: **1921**
Words: **316**
Sentences: **34**
Paragraphs: **20**
Show Less ▲

2. **Grammarly:** This tool checks your writing for grammar, spelling, and punctuation errors. It also offers suggestions to improve sentence structure and readability.

3. **Readable:** This tool analyzes your text for readability, providing scores and suggestions to improve clarity, simplicity, and engagement. It offers insights on factors such as sentence length, word choice, and use of transition words.

R readable

4. **Yoast SEO:** While primarily used for search engine optimization, Yoast SEO also offers a readability analysis for web content. It provides feedback on sentence structure, paragraph length, subheadings, and other factors that affect readability.

5. **Plain Language Checker:** This tool evaluates your writing for plain language, which is crucial for ensuring clarity and accessibility. It identifies jargon, long sentences, and other elements that may hinder comprehension.

Remember, while these tools can be helpful in assessing and improving readability, they should not be relied on exclusively. It's important to have a human editor or proofreader review your writing to ensure that it meets your audience's needs and goals.

Conclusion

From crafting effective microcopy to writing for complex interfaces, we have covered a range of topics to help you become a skilled UX writer. We have emphasized the importance of being user-centric, empathetic, and strategic in your writing approach.

The abundance of abstract data can be daunting at times, and stakeholders can only comprehend statistics and numerical information. Therefore, it is crucial to consider the most effective way to convey the message and simplify the data to ensure it is understood.

When conducting user research, it is essential to acquire both theoretical knowledge and practical skills to become proficient in all aspects of the process. The combination of theoretical knowledge and practical experience is the key to mastering the skills necessary to become a professional UX writer.

As you continue to refine your skills as a UX writer, keep in mind that the user is at the heart of everything you do. Your words have the power to guide and influence their actions and ultimately shape their experience with your product or service.

Stay curious and keep learning. The field of UX writing is constantly evolving, and there will always be new challenges to tackle and new opportunities to explore. Never stop experimenting and testing your writing to ensure that it's delivering the desired results.

Lastly, always remember that great UX writing is not just about using the right words, but also about crafting a cohesive and compelling narrative that tells the story of your product or service. By doing so, you can create experiences that are not only effective but also memorable and enjoyable for your users.

Glossary

1. A/B Testing - A method of comparing two versions of a product or design to determine which performs better. UX writers can use A/B testing to test different copy variations and see which one performs better with users.
2. Accessibility - The degree to which a product or service can be used by people with disabilities. UX writers should strive to create copy that is accessible to all users, regardless of their abilities.
3. Alt Text - Descriptive text that appears when an image fails to load or is not visible to a user. UX writers can create alt text that is concise and informative to help users understand the content of the image.
4. Analytics - The measurement and analysis of data related to user behavior on a website or app. UX writers can use analytics to understand how users interact with their copy and make data-driven decisions to improve it.
5. API Documentation - Documentation that explains how to use an API (Application Programming Interface). UX writers can create clear, concise

documentation to help developers understand how to integrate their product with other services.

6. Bounce Rate - The percentage of users who leave a website after viewing only one page. UX writers can reduce bounce rate by creating engaging and informative copy that encourages users to explore more of the site.

7. Call to Action (CTA) - A prompt that encourages users to take a specific action, such as clicking a button or filling out a form. UX writers can create effective CTAs by using clear and action-oriented language.

8. Content Audit - The process of evaluating and analyzing existing content to identify strengths, weaknesses, and opportunities for improvement. UX writers can conduct content audits to gain insights into user needs and preferences and to identify areas for improvement in their copy.

9. Content Marketing - The practice of creating and distributing content to attract and engage a target audience, with the goal of driving conversions and building brand awareness. UX writers can collaborate with marketing specialists to create copy that is effective for content marketing campaigns.

10. Content Strategy - The planning and management of content throughout its lifecycle, including creation, distribution, and measurement. Content strategy can help ensure that copy is effective, relevant, and engaging for users.

11. Contextual Help - Help content that is presented within the context of the user's current task. UX writers can create contextual help that provides users with the information they need at the moment they need it.

12. Copy - The words used in a product or design, including headlines, body copy, and labels. UX writers are responsible for creating copy that is clear, concise, and user-friendly.

13. Copy Testing - The process of testing copy with real users to evaluate its effectiveness, readability, and user experience. UX writers can use copy testing to gather feedback and insights on their copy and to identify areas for improvement.

14. CTA - See Call to Action.

15. Design System - A collection of reusable components, guidelines, and assets used to build consistent and cohesive products. UX writers can contribute to a design system by creating copy guidelines and voice and tone standards.

16. Error Message - A message that appears when a user encounters an error or issue while using a product. UX writers can create error messages that are clear, concise, and helpful in guiding the user to a solution.

17. Flow - The sequence of steps a user takes to complete a task or achieve a goal. UX writers can create copy that guides the user through the flow and helps them complete the task successfully.

18. Gated Content - Content that is hidden behind a form or paywall and requires the user to provide their information or payment details to access. UX writers can create copy that encourages users to provide their information and access the content.
19. Headline - The title or main text of a page or section. UX writers can create headlines that are clear, concise, and informative, and that encourage users to read on.
20. Information Architecture - The organization and structure of information within a product or design, including the hierarchy of content and the navigation system. UX writers can work with information architects to create an effective information architecture that supports their copy and helps users find what they need.
21. Interaction Design - The design of the interactive elements of a product or design, including buttons, forms, and other interface elements. UX writers can work with interaction designers to create effective and intuitive interactions that support their copy.
22. Localization - The process of adapting copy for different languages and cultures, including the use of appropriate language, tone, and cultural references. UX writers can work with localization specialists to ensure that their copy is effective and culturally sensitive for users in different regions.
23. Microcopy - Short, concise copy used to provide guidance or feedback to users, such as button labels

or error messages. UX writers can create effective microcopy that is clear, concise, and user-friendly.

24. Multimedia Content - Content that includes multiple forms of media, such as images, videos, and audio. UX writers can collaborate with multimedia specialists to create effective multimedia content that supports their copy and enhances the user experience.

25. Onboarding - The process of introducing new users to a product or service. UX writers can create onboarding copy that guides the user through the process and helps them understand how to use the product.

26. Persona - A fictional representation of a user type or group, used to help understand and design for the user's needs and goals. UX writers can create personas that accurately represent the target audience and inform their writing decisions.

27. Persuasive Writing - The practice of creating copy that persuades users to take a specific action or change their behavior, such as making a purchase or signing up for a service. UX writers can use persuasive language and techniques to create copy that is effective for conversion optimization and user engagement.

28. Plain Language - Clear and concise language that is easy to understand for all users, regardless of their background or education level. UX writers can use plain language to improve the accessibility and

readability of their copy and to reduce user confusion and frustration.

29. Prototype - A preliminary version of a product or design used for testing and evaluation. UX writers can create copy for prototypes that accurately reflects the final product and provides a realistic user experience.

30. Readability - The ease with which text can be read and understood. UX writers should aim to create copy that is easily readable and comprehensible to users of all literacy levels.

31. SEO - Search Engine Optimization, the process of optimizing a website or content to rank higher in search engine results pages. UX writers can create copy that incorporates relevant keywords and is structured in a way that is easily crawled and indexed by search engines.

32. Style Guide - A set of guidelines and standards for creating consistent and cohesive content across a product or brand. UX writers can contribute to a style guide by creating guidelines for voice and tone, grammar, and punctuation.

33. Surveys - A method of collecting feedback and information from users through a series of questions. UX writers can use surveys to gather user feedback on their copy and make improvements based on user responses.

34. Task Analysis - The process of breaking down a task into smaller steps to understand how users complete

it. UX writers can use task analysis to create copy that guides the user through the task and helps them complete it successfully.

35. Typography - The style, size, and arrangement of text in a product or design. UX writers can contribute to typography by creating guidelines for font usage, spacing, and hierarchy.

36. User Flow - See Flow.

37. User Interface (UI) - The visual and interactive elements of a product or design that users interact with, including buttons, forms, and other interface elements. UX writers can work with designers and developers to create UI elements that are easy to understand and use.

38. User Persona - See Persona.

39. User Research - The process of gathering and analyzing data about user behavior, needs, and goals to inform product design decisions. UX writers can contribute to user research by conducting user interviews and surveys to understand how users interact with their copy.

40. User Testing - The process of testing a product or design with users to evaluate its effectiveness and identify areas for improvement. UX writers can conduct user testing to gather feedback on their copy and make improvements based on user responses.

41. Visual Design - The design of the visual elements of a product or design, including color, typography, and

layout. UX writers can work with visual designers to create a cohesive and effective design that supports their copy.

42. Voice and Tone - The personality and style of a brand or product, including the language and messaging used in the copy. UX writers can create guidelines for voice and tone that align with the brand's values and resonate with the target audience.

43. White Space - The empty space around and between design elements, used to create visual balance and focus. UX writers can use white space to enhance the readability and visual appeal of their copy.

44. Wireframe - A visual representation of a product or design, used for planning and communication purposes. UX writers can work with designers and other team members to create wireframes that accurately reflect the final product and provide a realistic user experience.

45. Wireframing - The process of creating a preliminary visual representation of a product or design, used for planning and communication purposes. UX writers can collaborate with designers and other team members to create wireframes that accurately reflect the final product and provide a realistic user experience.

46. Word Choice - The selection of appropriate words to convey a message effectively and accurately. UX writers should consider the connotations and

associations of words when choosing them for their copy.

47. Writing for Accessibility - The practice of creating copy that is accessible to users with disabilities, including the use of clear language, descriptive text for images, and other techniques to make content perceivable, operable, and understandable to all users. UX writers can collaborate with accessibility specialists to create copy that is inclusive and accessible to all users.

48. Writing for Calls-to-Action (CTAs) - The practice of creating copy that encourages users to take specific actions, such as clicking a button or filling out a form. UX writers can use clear and compelling language to create effective CTAs that drive user engagement and conversions.

49. Writing for Clarity - The practice of creating copy that is clear and easily understood by users. UX writers can use simple language, avoid jargon and technical terms, and organize their copy in a logical and intuitive way to enhance clarity.

50. Writing for Conversions - The practice of creating copy that persuades users to take a specific action, such as making a purchase or signing up for a service. UX writers can use persuasive language, calls to action, and other techniques to optimize their copy for conversions.

51. Writing for Engagement - The practice of creating copy that engages users and encourages them to

interact with a product or design. UX writers can use storytelling, humor, and other techniques to make their copy more engaging and compelling.

52. Writing for Error Messages - The practice of creating clear and concise copy for error messages, helping users understand what went wrong and how to fix it. UX writers can use empathetic language and clear instructions to reduce user frustration and improve the user experience.

53. Writing for Internationalization - The practice of creating copy that can be easily translated into other languages and cultures. UX writers can use simple and straightforward language, avoid cultural references, and adhere to best practices for internationalization to ensure that their copy is easily translatable.

54. Writing for Microcopy - The practice of creating short, concise, and actionable copy for small interface elements such as buttons, labels, and tooltips. UX writers can use microcopy to provide guidance, feedback, and other useful information to users.

55. Writing for Mobile Content - The practice of creating copy that is optimized for mobile devices, including the use of concise language, clear headings, and other techniques to enhance readability and usability. UX writers can collaborate with mobile designers and developers to create copy that is

effective on small screens and in different mobile contexts.

56. Writing for Navigation - The practice of creating copy that helps users navigate a product or design. UX writers can use clear and descriptive labels, instructions, and other techniques to make navigation intuitive and easy for users.

57. Writing for Onboarding - The practice of creating copy that guides new users through the process of getting started with a product or design. UX writers can use clear and concise instructions, examples, and other techniques to make onboarding easy and effective for users.

58. Writing for Personalization - The practice of creating copy that is tailored to individual users based on their preferences, behavior, and other factors. UX writers can use dynamic content, personalization tokens, and other techniques to make their copy more relevant and engaging for users.

59. Writing for SEO - The practice of creating copy that is optimized for search engines, including the use of keywords and other techniques to improve search engine rankings. UX writers can collaborate with SEO specialists to create copy that is both user-friendly and search engine-friendly.

60. Writing for Social Media - The practice of creating copy that is optimized for social media platforms, including the use of hashtags, emojis, and other techniques to increase engagement and reach. UX

writers can collaborate with social media specialists to create copy that resonates with their target audience.

61. Writing for Usability - The practice of creating copy that enhances the usability of a product or design. UX writers can use clear and concise language, avoid ambiguity and confusion, and follow best practices for usability to ensure that their copy is user-friendly and effective.

62. Writing for User Education - The practice of creating copy that teaches users how to use a product or design effectively. UX writers can use tutorials, how-to guides, and other educational content to help users learn and master complex tasks and features.

63. Writing for User Experience - The practice of creating copy that enhances the overall user experience of a product or design. UX writers can use storytelling, emotion, and other techniques to create a memorable and engaging user experience.

64. Writing for Voice Assistants - The practice of creating copy that is optimized for voice assistants, including the use of natural language and other techniques to create a conversational experience. UX writers can collaborate with developers and voice design specialists to create copy that is effective for voice-based interactions.

65. Writing for Web Content - The practice of creating copy that is optimized for web content, including the use of headings, bullet points, and other techniques

to enhance readability and usability. UX writers can work with web designers and developers to create copy that is both user-friendly and visually appealing.

66. Writing Guidelines - A set of guidelines and standards for creating consistent and cohesive copy across a product or brand. UX writers can contribute to writing guidelines by creating guidelines for voice and tone, grammar, and punctuation.

67. Writing Process - The process of creating copy, including planning, drafting, editing, and revising. UX writers can follow a structured writing process to ensure that their copy is effective, efficient, and meets the needs of their users.

68. Writing Style - The style and format of copy, including the use of voice and tone, grammar, punctuation, and other stylistic elements. UX writers can use a consistent writing style to create a cohesive user experience across a product or brand.

69. Writing Voice - The personality and tone of the copy, reflecting the brand and its values. UX writers can use a consistent writing voice to create a unique and memorable brand identity and to connect with their users.

Discover the <u>Easiest and Fastest</u> Way to Learn UX writing as a complete Beginner with step-by-step Guidance For career development!

On sale at Amazon.com